What's My Excuse

For Not Being a Christian?

12 Myths of Christianity

Brad Crouser

with kindest regards,
Brad Crouser

Publisher's Cataloging-in-Publication
(Provided by Quality Books, Inc.)

Crouser, Brad.
 What's my excuse? for not being a Christian : 12 myths of Christianity / by Brad Crouser
 p. cm.
 Includes index.
 LCCN 2004105260
 ISBN 0-9724867-5-5

 1. Jesus Christ--Historicity. 2. Apologetics.
I. Title.

BT303.2.C76 2004   232.9'08
              QBI04-700175

Copyright © 2004 Brad Crouser
ISBN 0-9724867-5-5

All rights reserved. Written permission must be secured from the publisher to use or reproduce any part of this book in any form or by any means – graphic, electronic, or mechanical, including photocopying, recording, taping, or by any information storage retrieval system — except for brief quotations in critical reviews or articles.

Scripture taken from the HOLY BIBLE, NEW INTERNATIONAL VERSION, Copyright (c) 1973, 1978, 1984 International Bible Society. Used by permission of Zondervan Bible Publishers.

Published In Beautiful West Virginia By Woodland Gospel Publishing
A Division Of Woodland Press, LLC
www.woodlandgospel.com
SAN: 2 5 4 - 9 9 9 9

To
F. Raamie Barker,
*friend, mentor and brother in Christ,
who helped to make this
book possible*

CONTENTS

INTRODUCTION
7

MYTH 1:
JESUS NEVER CLAIMED TO BE GOD
13

MYTH 2:
THERE WAS NO RESURRECTION
27

MYTH 3:
JESUS' MISSION WAS TO BE A TEACHER
39

MYTH 4:
THE CHURCH IS FULL OF HYPOCRITES
51

MYTH 5:
I'D NEED TO CLEAN UP MY LIFE TO BECOME A CHRISTIAN
59

MYTH 6:
ALL CHURCHES ARE ALIKE
69

MYTH 7:
EVERYTHING CLAIMING TO BE CHRISTIAN REALLY IS
83

MYTH 8:
CHRISTIANITY IS JUST LIKE OTHER RELIGIONS
99

MYTH 9:
CHRISTIANITY IS FOR LOSERS
107

MYTH 10:
CHRISTIANITY ISN'T FAIR!
117

MYTH 11:
CHRISTIANS AREN'T SUPPOSED TO HAVE FUN
125

MYTH 12:
THE BIBLE TEACHES THIS WORLD IS COMING TO AN END
137

CONCLUSION
ALTAR CALL
145

INTRODUCTION

With few exceptions, the religious beliefs of most of us who have lived on this planet have been chosen for us, before we were born. More than anything else, the geographical location of birth and the religion of our parents have dictated the beliefs and creeds of the great majority of us.

For centuries, the few existing Bibles in most European towns were owned by the churches, often chained to the pulpits and usually in Latin. But it didn't matter what language they were written in, because most parishioners were illiterate, anyway. For that and other reasons, they relied upon the clergy to tell them what the scriptures said and to interpret their meaning.

With the advent of the printing press, and the proliferation of Bibles translated into native tongues, people in the West had a better opportunity to begin thinking for themselves. They could come to their own conclusions and challenge the dogma of the church leadership. As we know, that newfound access to information helped fuel the fires of the Protestant Reformation.

The reformers' goal of a return to sound, accurate Christian doctrine has proven to be elusive, however. While the established Roman Catholic Church quite obviously was full of error, corrupt and desperately crying for drastic change, the Protestant movement immediately began fragmenting into many contrary, opposing doctrines. Many of these new church leaders also would go off on doctrinal tangents, far from Biblical truth. Some were uneducated or had ill motives. The result is that today there are thousands of quite varied and diverse denominations calling themselves Christian.

So with the good, then, came the bad, and not just the faulty theology and occasional heresies that occurred in the "reformed" churches. The Modern Era's "higher criticism" dared to challenge the veracity of the Bible itself. Seeds of skepticism — of anything supernatural, doubt that there were ever miracles or anything that could not be experienced with our senses here and now — were sown among those who once trusted the Scriptures. The theory of evolution began squeezing out the belief in a Divine Creator — at least the One portrayed in Genesis — and has become religious dogma in itself, not to be challenged.

Our present Postmodern Era is more tolerant of spirituality, realizing there is an unfilled void without it. But it eschews any belief system claiming to be the *only* valid one. Its "child," political correctness, tolerates anything but that which smacks of intolerance. It holds that, whatever works for you is acceptable, equally valid as the next guy's beliefs, since ultimate truth is unknowable, anyway. The only "sin" recognized in Postmodernism is the "bigotry" of people like Christians, who claim that Jesus is the exclusive way to God, true peace, wisdom and eternal life.

To many of this age, as in the Apostle Paul's era, the Christian gospel (the good news) is absolute "foolishness." The very concept — of God, the Creator of the universe, on earth in the form of a man, allowing Himself to be executed on a cross to pay the sin debt of humankind, arising from the dead, and giving eternal life to those who will accept Him as their Lord (boss) and Savior (deliverer from Hell) — is just preposterous. To them it's not a "respectable" or credible philosophy. It's something only uneducated, unsophisticated, easily-lead, gullible people would accept.

But Paul quotes God's pronouncement in Isaiah 29:14, "I will destroy the wisdom of the wise; the intelligence of the intelligent I will frustrate." The gospel might be foolishness to "those who are perishing," Paul writes, "but to us who are being saved it is the power of God." Think what you will, smart guy, says Paul, but it's working for us!

For that reason, one of my law partners suggested that I call this book *Foolish Wisdom*. "But God chose the foolish things of the world to shame the wise," Paul wrote. He was referring not only to the "simple" gospel message, but also to the weak, lowly and despised people who often were chosen by Jesus to build His kingdom, including fishermen, prostitutes and tax collectors. Notice that He did not call the political, educational or religious leaders of the day. To demonstrate that salvation is of God, a gift by grace, not earned, Jesus said that God even *hides* "these things from the [worldly] wise and learned, and reveal[s] them to little children."

What you are reading is somewhat unique. This author is not a theologian. I did not attend a seminary. This is a "lay" book, written by a "layman," written for others without a formal Bible education. In fact, before it became a book, originally this was a private project, written to convince an intellectual agnostic of the veracity of the gospel.

Did it convince him? I'm sorry to say it did not. But where there is life there is hope, right? Without the convicting power of the Holy Spirit, to show us that our sins are great, that they separate us from God, and that we need a Savior, no one is ever saved. The best logic and argument will never persuade him.

But you know what? I have more respect for someone who says, "I know what Christianity is about, but I just don't want to be one," than for the type which is more commonly seen. More typical among those who have heard the gospel is the one who makes a shallow, superficial commitment to Christ that is actually worthless, even dangerous, to his soul. Many "come forward" in a church service, have an emotional experience, sign a card, get baptized or perform some ritual, join or even participate in a church, get their consciences soothed, all the time fooling themselves into thinking they are true Christians, when they are not.

Unless their conversion was genuine, they are no more a real

Christian than is an atheist. It is that large group of self-deluded who will be eternally shocked and disappointed when they stand before Jesus at Judgment, to be told to depart from Him because He never knew them. They hadn't done "the will of the Father who is in Heaven." They lulled themselves to sleep, thinking they'd procured eternal life by simply augmenting Jesus to their lifestyles in some casual way, like joining a club.

But what He requires is something far more radical than that. Essentially, Jesus calls upon us to give up our own lives and take on His own, a 100% commitment. Like signing up for the military, He wants people who are willing to go where He sends them, do whatever He requests, when He demands it. Wrote Billy Graham:

> *It is only when we come to the will that we find the very heart of repentance. There must be that determination to forsake sin — to change one's attitude toward self, toward sin, and God; to change one's feeling: to change one's will, disposition, and purpose ... There is not one verse of Scripture that indicates that you can be a Christian and live any kind of life you want to.*†

And with that transformation, we accept some of the same difficulties and persecutions Jesus had to endure on this earth. He warned that we'd have to take up our own crosses to follow Him. It is not something to be entered into without thought and consideration of the cost, He often emphasized. He compared it to having enough materials to construct a building, enough troops to win a battle, and plowing an entire field. If we're going to follow him, Jesus wants us to go all the way: a full effort, an entire lifetime, unwavering.

His is a very narrow way, Jesus also explained, and few would actually enter into it. The crowds loved His words, His miracles and the food He sometimes provided, but thousands rejected and refused His invitation to discipleship during His three-year ministry, once they understood what He was demanding. A small handful, probably 500 or less, actually became His true followers. Some, like the Rich Young Ruler, went away saddened when they learned that they had to make Him Christ of their lives, surrendering their worldly goals, idols and riches to become His disciples. He most certainly did not offer "easy believism" just to swell His crowds.

So it is better to determine if Christianity is true, and then determine if you're really willing to become a follower of Christ, before "joining up."

But what one receives, in exchange for surrendering his short life here (giving up what he can't keep, anyway) in order to accept Christ, is of *immeasurable value*, He promises. In Matthew 13:46, Jesus compares it to selling everything you own to buy a "pearl of great price." He urgently tells us to destroy, sever anything that would keep us from following Him. In Matthew 5:29, He even urges one to cut off a body part, pluck out an eye, whatever it takes to abandon a sinful lifestyle, turn from earthly pursuits, and become a commited follower. He makes it clear there is a "tradeoff," a sacrifice of our lives, but we get an infinitely good bargain out of "the deal."

And the best part is that He will not reject any who come to Him in true repentance. "Everyone who looks to the Son and believes in Him shall have eternal life," Jesus promises in John 6:40, it being the will of God the Father.

A few who've previewed the following chapters complain that I have tried to "prove Scripture by quoting Scripture." And that's true, to an extent. I must confess, I simply know of no better way to make these arguments.

I am convinced that the Bible was written by men who were directly inspired by God and, in the case of the four Gospels, actually were reliable eyewitnesses to the events they describe.

There are numerous scholarly books which successfully (I think) poke holes into the theory of evolution. Many books have been written which demonstrate the flaws and futility of other world religions. We could examine the results of archeological digs, artifacts and early scrolls, which give credence to the authenticity of Christianity. As others have done, we could list hundreds of prophecies that have been fulfilled, validating the Bible. But, would any of that really prove that the Gospel is true?

No, Christ stands as He always has, to be believed or disbelieved, accepted or rejected — you must decide. We must choose this day whom we will serve. As Paul wrote in Romans 1:16: *I am not ashamed of the gospel, because it is the power of God for the salvation of everyone who believes.*

And the Bible, says the writer of Hebrews, is "sharper than any double-edged sword," penetrating the soul and judging our thoughts and attitudes. If we trust it to be the inspired Word of God, then it is an immeasurably valuable asset, of great power, providing ultimate wisdom.

Some say, "Oh, I don't believe in a literal Hell." Others may have their own version of God: a loving, tolerant, grandfatherly image. None of that "wrath and judgment stuff" in their theology. They give the Bible little credibility. But I ask, upon what do *you* base your views? Is it reliable enough to risk your eternal future?

So, jumping into the scriptures, the only reliable source I can locate, we'll try to address several questions/objections/misconceptions many have when confronted with the choice of accepting or rejecting Jesus Christ as their Lord and Savior. Perhaps these will be useful to a nonbeliever in making a decision. Or it may simply reassure what a believing reader already knows to be true.

If you're looking for light reading with amusing anecdotes, I'm sorry — this is probably not for you. We're going to discuss some serious business here. Issues of eternal consequence. Hopefully, some life-changing concepts.

MYTH 1:
JESUS NEVER CLAIMED TO BE GOD

Christianity has always stood on two legs: the first, that Jesus is God; the second, that He arose from the dead. If you knock out either or both of these assumptions, it collapses. It becomes just another philosophy, powerless to save or change lives.

A recurring attack upon the key, central doctrine of Christianity — that Jesus of Nazareth is God Incarnate — has always been around. Not only among nonbelievers, but even in the Church itself and in so-called Christian seminaries, are many who say, "Jesus was a great, wise teacher, but even He did not pretend to be divine; He was just an enlightened man."

Even Nicodemus, a member of the hostile Pharisees, conceded that his group knew that Jesus was "a teacher who has come from God." Brilliant men throughout history, including Benjamin Franklin, Thomas Jefferson, Albert Einstein and Mahatma Gandhi, saluted Jesus as an historic figure, a special moral leader. They even quoted Him, but stopped far short of suggesting that He is God.

Today many Hindus, Buddhists, Muslims, New Agers, and even some Jews, among others, will accept that there was a Jesus who was possibly a prophet, likely "ahead of His time," drawing upon wisdom and mysticism that existed before His age. They admit that He taught great moral rules and lessons of life. But, generally, they refuse to concede that He was any more of a god than you or me.

A CRITICAL QUESTION

Our lifespan here on earth is a mere vapor, as James 4:14 and Psalm 39:5 point out. Very few of us live for more than seven to nine short decades. Obviously, eternity is forever; it is difficult to even conceive of a never-ending existence. So, if there is an eternal existence hereafter, then it goes without saying that it is extremely important for us to consider our destiny.

Consequently, no question could be more important to humankind: Was this Jesus of Nazareth, a carpenter and itinerate preacher, truly a visitation by God in flesh, upon the earth for about 33 years?

If not, then millions of His followers sadly have been duped; they have been wasting their time for 2000 years worshiping a heretic. But if it's even a possibility, then learning of Him, His example of living, the lessons that He taught us, the commands He gave, His explanations of God the Father, and His predictions regarding future events, is of the utmost importance — don't you agree?

Let's suppose for a moment that some advanced, brilliant creature from another solar system visited earth for a few years and imparted his or her wisdom to us. Wouldn't every word be recorded and studied for centuries?

How much more important is it, then, if the Creator of the universe sent a part of Himself, His Son, to be with us? At the very least, should we not study diligently to determine whether Jesus really was the Son of God, deity come to earth? Shouldn't we at least read what He had to say? In other words, can we safely ignore such an enormous issue? Shouldn't we resolve it in our own minds, once and for all? Isn't such an important subject worth at least some investigative time?

ABUNDANT DOCUMENTATION

If we accept as valid the primary source of the history and utterances of Jesus — the four Gospels — what can we learn from them with regard to the subject of whether or not He was deity? Did He claim to be God, as the Christians contend, or did Jesus refrain from taking the mantle of Godhood, as many non-believers maintain?

Even a quick study of this subject provides surprising results. There are numerous references throughout the four Gospels alone, written by contemporaries of Jesus, offering proof that He was the Messiah, not just "The Son of David," or "The Anointed One," but actually the Son of the Living God, deity in flesh, of the exact same divine sum and substance as the Creator of the universe.

FORETOLD THROUGH THE PROPHETS

Even hundreds of years prior to the Gospels being recorded, the Prophet Isaiah predicted that the Messiah would be called Immanuel, meaning "God with us." Isaiah also predicted that the Messiah would be the "Mighty God" and the "Everlasting Father." By these titles he explained that the Messiah was to be One who is far greater, infinitely more significant than a mere political or religious leader, as had been expected by most of the Jews for centuries. The Prophet Micah said that the Messiah's "goings forth have been from of old, from everlasting," indicating that the Messiah would be one who had existed in eternity past, unlike mere mortals. (Keep in mind that the Jews accepted the prophets' words as direct revelation from God.)

WHAT DID JESUS CLAIM?

While it is true that Jesus did not always fully disclose His divine identity while on earth, and sometimes even warned His followers not to reveal it, there were many other times when He plainly claimed to be God in the flesh. While He often referred to Himself in third person, His listeners had no doubt that He was speaking of Himself and no one else.

Jesus, nor His followers, nor the authors of the New Testament books, ever explained how one could be fully man and fully God at the same time. That paradox has been debated, even inside the Church, for centuries. However, the New Testament contends that Jesus was exactly that.

If we believe Matthew, a former tax collector for the Roman government (who gave away his considerable wealth to follow Jesus), no less than God the Father audibly proclaimed Jesus' identity when He was baptized by John the Baptist, in a voice that was heard by those present, "This is my Son, whom I love, with Him I am well pleased." Matthew reports that God the Father later reaffirmed that proclamation at the Transfiguration, as witnessed by the Apostles Peter, James and John.

THE SON OF GOD

Throughout the four Gospels, Jesus often referred to God as "My Father," claiming a special relationship shared by none other. He often referred to Himself as *"the* Son of Man," a slightly different and higher title than God used to address the prophet Ezekiel and a title the prophet Daniel had used for the pre-incarnate Christ he had seen. Jesus did not call Himself *"a* Son of Man," which would translate to "a human being," no greater than you and me. The term "Son of Man" was widely accepted in First Century Palestine as the term for the Messiah, the Christ, the Anointed One, the Son of God.

He also referred to Himself as Lord, and spoke of Himself as the Judge humankind will face at the Last Judgment. He plainly told the Jewish leaders of the day that He had "authority on earth to forgive sins," and indicated that He even had the authority to choose those to be saved. Jesus told Thomas, His disciple, that He is *the* way, *the* truth and *the* life, and that no one comes to God the Father except through Him. If those statements were not a claim to deity, it is difficult to imagine exactly what else would be!

Jesus freely proclaimed Himself to be superior to the Jewish law and even that He fulfilled the Law. When the rich young ruler addressed Him as being "good," Jesus inferred that this man had called Him God, because "there is only One who is good." On many occasions, the Gospels record that Jesus allowed people to worship Him, something He would not have done had He denied His deity.

Interestingly, the Gospels make it clear that Jesus did not wish to go around simply claiming to be God. After all, anyone could do that; others before and after Him had done so. Rather, it appears that Jesus wanted individuals to observe what He did, as well as what He said, and thus allow them to draw their own conclusions. It almost seems at times that He intended to obscure His identity, possibly to hide it from those whom God had not chosen for eternal life. He did not then, nor does He now, reveal Himself to everyone, for reasons we do not fully comprehend.

PROVEN BY MIRACLES

His deity was demonstrated by His ability to perform unduplicated miracles, time and time again. Jesus admitted that He performed the miracles primarily to prove His identity to the world. That is why the record of His miracles are so important and why it is so wrong to ignore them. America's third president revealed his complete ignorance of Jesus' true nature by deleting references to the miraculous from his so-called "Jefferson Bible" that he prepared for the Native Americans. Those miracles revealed Jesus' compassion and character but, more importantly, displayed supernatural power that no mere mortal has ever possessed. He proved that He could instantly raise the dead, heal the sick, blind and lame, and that He even had power over weather and nature itself.

Note, interestingly, that Jesus' contemporary critics did not deny that He performed these miracles. From among the ranks of His enemies, the Pharisees, Nicodemus acknowledged that Jesus had come from God because of the "miraculous signs" He had performed. Instead, some of them simply attributed His supernatural powers to Satan. Those leaders feared losing their political and religious power because of the impact His miracles had upon the populace. They had selfish motivation to discredit Him, but they would have appeared to be fools if they'd denied that miracles were occurring. The masses knew that Jesus was performing miracles; thousands had witnessed them. That's why most followed Him. They had among them people who had been healed — even restored to life — testifying to His power. There was no denying it.

Indeed, when John the Baptizer — his faith challenged as he lay in prison awaiting his beheading — inquired as to whether Jesus was truly the "One who is to come," as John had previously proclaimed to the multitudes, Jesus responded by pointing to His miracles as proof that He was the One who was prophesied, the Messiah, the Son of God.

OMNISCIENT AND OMNIPRESENT

Another way Jesus proved that He was not merely a wise teacher was through His omniscience. The Gospels are replete with references to the prophesies of Jesus, His reading of people's minds, His description of Heaven and Hell as if He had personally seen both (He had), and having a perfect, authoritative response to every question thrown at Him. His mind reflected the omniscience of His Heavenly Father because He was in perfect union with Him.

In His resurrected form, Jesus shocked His followers by His omnipresence, by being able to travel instantaneously, to appear in many places within a very short period of time, and to even be able to walk through locked doors. No mere mortal has ever been able to do that in recorded history, only in science fiction.

REVEALING HIMSELF

Direct self-disclosure of His divine identity was rarely recorded. One rare example was when Jesus disclosed to the Samaritan women at the well that He was the Messiah. Jesus also confessed His deity to the man He healed of blindness.

It was not until Jesus was near the day of His crucifixion that He began to confirm to His close followers what He had actually proven by His words, deeds and miracles during His ministry. He at last asked His disciples, "Who do people say the Son of Man is?" referring to Himself. They responded that many of His contemporaries thought that He was one of the Jewish prophets, back from the dead. But when He pressed, "Who do *you* say I am?" Simon Peter, the boldest of the twelve, shouted, "You are the Christ [the Messiah]," adding, "the Son of the Living God."

Jesus, you will carefully note, did not refute such a statement or scold Peter for blaspheming, as would be expected if he had made a false statement and Jesus was but a "wise teacher." Moreover, He did not correct Peter by saying, "I am *a* god," as Hindus or New Agers might accept. To the contrary, He confirmed that Peter was correct, stating that such a revelation was not of human origin, but had been disclosed to Peter by God the Father. (And even today, that principle remains: Christ' identity must be revealed to us by the Holy Spirit in order for us to accept and understand His deity.)

Jesus told another of His disciples, Philip, "...I am in the Father and ... the Father is in me," explaining that it was God in Him who was "doing His work." When another disciple, Thomas, cried out to Him, "My Lord and my God!" in recognition of His deity after His resurrection, Jesus not only accepted his acknowledgment but commended his belief.

HIS ENEMIES UNDERSTOOD HIS CLAIMS

The First Century Jewish religious leaders not only had tremendous political power in Palestine, but great wealth and the respect of the people. As mentioned, they had the most to lose if this Jesus guy was really the long-prophesied Messiah, because what He was saying and doing was surely going to "upset their applecart." He wasn't coming to augment their role, and He wasn't playing their game. To the contrary, they were out of step with Jesus' New Covenant. According to John 5:18, they knew exactly who He was claiming to be and that is why they sought to kill Him. Their chief complaint was that Jesus was blaspheming; they charged that He, a mere man, was claiming to be equal to God. They may have strongly disagreed with that claim, but there is never any indication that the Jewish leaders doubted that Jesus was claiming to be the Son of God.

A First Century secular historian, Josephus, twice wrote that Jesus of Nazareth was considered to be the Christ, so His claims were understood even by non-religious contemporaries.

Jesus had explained to the Pharisees through Scripture that the Messiah, although a descendent in the line of King David, would be more than simply the Son of David, because (in the Psalms) David had actually called Him "Lord."

The Jewish leadership also wanted to kill Jesus because He had taken authority over the Temple area, twice clearing it of the corrupt money-changers, again, displaying authority not given by man. Indeed, even as a twelve-year-old, Jesus had referred to the Temple, in which God was believed to dwell, as "*my* Father's house." (Emphasis added.)

Jesus told the Jewish leaders that He "came from God and now am here." When He told them, "before Abraham was born, *I am!*" they knew exactly what He meant; He was not simply making a grammatical error. "I am" was the very name of God Himself, you see. And, for that claim, the Jewish leaders tried to stone Jesus to death at the Temple for blasphemy. He also told them, directly, "I and the Father are One," and that "the Father is in Me and I in the Father," for which they again tried to execute Him on the spot.

Indeed, the "I am" utterance was so powerful that, when Jesus proclaimed it at the time of His arrest in the garden, soldiers actually fell to the ground, according to a witness. At His trial before the Sanhedrin, Jesus was asked directly by His religious court inquisitors whether He was claiming to be the Christ, the Son of God. He replied affirmatively, promising that in the future they would see Him sitting at the right hand of God (the most honored position) and coming on the clouds of Heaven. Again, there was no question that they understood His meaning. The high priest tore his clothing in outrage, called Him a blasphemer and condemned Him to death for the statement.

Likewise, when Pilate, the Roman governor appointed by Caesar, questioned Him at His trial, Jesus confirmed His claim that He was the King of the Jews, as accused by the Jewish leadership. But, according to John's Gospel, Jesus also explained to Pilate that His "Kingdom [was] from another place." Thus, Pilate understood that Jesus was then claiming a spiritual monarchy, not leadership of a political or military kingdom. Had it been the latter, Pilate would have been required under Roman law to condemn Him to death as a dangerous revolutionary. There had been several political "messiahs" in Palestine, before and after Jesus, who were put to death because the Roman government feared a revolt by the Jews, which did eventually occur circa 70 A.D. But Pilate understood perfectly Jesus' meaning; he acquitted Him and even wanted to release Jesus after this courtroom exchange. Pilate insisted upon the posted inscription, "Jesus of Nazareth, the King of the Jews," to be fastened to Jesus' cross and refused to modify it upon demand of the outraged Jewish leaders. It seems that Pilate may have been persuaded. Perhaps his wife's revelatory dream the night before the trial had something to do with that.

DID HIS FOLLOWERS "INVENT" HIS DEITY?

Was Jesus' deity simply a fabrication by His followers, something they invented to justify their "cult," as some accuse?

Even most skeptics will admit that the authors of the Gospels likely recorded Jesus' words as close to verbatim as possible, in the Jewish tradition of that time relating to the words spoken by a prophet or an important rabbi. Undoubtedly, John and Matthew had heard Jesus repeat the same basic sermon to groups in different locales, re-enforcing their memorization of His words. Dr. Luke's quotes also are believed to be verbatim and some think that Mark's Gospel might have been dictated by Peter, who heard it all firsthand. Of course, Christians believe that the Gospels' authors were inspired in their writings by the Holy Spirit.

Their preaching and written recordings began almost immediately after the crucifixion. The Church, within weeks of that event, began to grow by the thousands because they knew those words were true. The growth would not have occurred so soon had the people of Palestine, Jesus' contemporaries, known it to be a lie.

Did the authors of the New Testament have "an agenda," part of which was to prove the divinity of Jesus? No question about it! The Apostle John repeats over and over again, in both his Gospel and in First John, his purpose for writing: that we might *believe* in Jesus.

But does that agenda make these books and letters untrue? Of course not! *All* literature, ancient or modern, has "an agenda," either consciously or unconsciously, whether it be to record facts, inform, educate, persuade or entertain.

It is amazing that so many people will accept without question other ancient manuscripts as being true and valid but discount the Gospels and the writings of the New Testament authors as simple, superstitious, religious myths. In their minds, the Bible is fable until proven otherwise. But, quite frankly, the burden is upon them to prove these documents false; they stand undisputed by any contemporaneous source. These were not fables invented hundreds of years later, as with myths or other religions; the reports were made at a time when potential rebuttal witnesses were still living, in the First Century, and could refute them if untrue. No contemporaneous document has been discovered that does that.

CAN THEIR CLAIMS BE TRUSTED?

Possibly the most convincing argument for the validity of the books written by Matthew, Mark, Luke, John, Paul, James, Peter and the other New Testament authors is the fact that, almost without exception, all of these authors were tortured mercilessly (whipped, stoned, imprisoned, etc.), lost family and friends, suffered tremendous personal and financial loss throughout their lifetimes, and ended up dying cruel deaths, usually through execution, due solely to the message they were preaching (that Jesus was God and that He rose from the dead). In most cases, all they had to do to avoid that persecution was to renounce their claim that Jesus of Nazareth was God. They could have safely reverted to their Jewish traditions and religious rites, escaping persecution.

But the true believers refused to do so, knowing the Gospel ("the Good News") to be true and factual. It was such an astounding, powerful message that they could not keep from telling it to thousands of people. They certainly could not deny it, even at the risk of losing their own lives. For it is one thing for an individual to die as the result of mistakenly believing and proclaiming a lie, as millions of martyrs from other religions and political beliefs have done over the centuries. But to suffer and die for something you know to be a *lie* is absolutely unheard of. No sane person would do that. The first Church knew it was not a lie and that's why they risked everything, including their own lives, to spread the Gospel. They certainly received no earthly reward for preaching it, only suffering and shame.

That is probably why God did not allow any of the early disciples of Jesus, particularly the apostles, to be wealthy. That is probably why He allowed them to suffer torture, humiliation, and imprisonment throughout their lifetimes and to die as martyrs. He knew that even their lives would be proof that they were not building an empire, not getting rich by spreading this "new religion," and they certainly were not winning popularity or favor from the Establishment of that time. What they were proclaiming, at tremendous peril to themselves, their families and fellow believers, was *the Truth*. No one has ever been able to demonstrate that those early leaders of the Church had any ulterior motive for preaching Christ and winning converts.

The followers of Jesus had witnessed this miraculous life, death and resurrection with their own eyes and could not be quiet about it. Observe, when Peter preached his first sermon to the 3,000 in Jerusalem after Pentecost, there is no record of anyone denying that what he alleged was untrue. No one denied that Jesus was the Son of God or denied that He'd risen from the dead only a few weeks before that sermon. Instead, Peter's large audience became converts! This "new religion" had been launched, based upon a true claim, a firm foundation, not myth or speculation. Their claims of Jesus' deity were, and are, reliable.

WHAT WILL YOU DO WITH JESUS?

There has been no better summation of this question of Jesus' deity than that made several decades ago by the brilliant Oxford professor and prolific author, C.S. Lewis. In his book *Mere Christianity*, Lewis tried to dispel the notion that Jesus was a great leader but not God. In a classic summation, Lewis wrote that a man who said the sort of things Jesus said would not be a "great moral teacher" if He was merely a man. He would either be a deluded lunatic, "the Devil of Hell," or exactly whom He claimed to be, the Son of God. So each must make a choice, Lewis continued. Either dismiss Jesus as a fool, scorn Him as an evil figure, or fall and worship Him as Thomas did. But Jesus did not leave open to us "any patronizing nonsense about His being a great human teacher."

So this same question looms before everyone today, just as it has for 2000 years: Was Jesus of Nazareth a divine being, man and God in combination, or was He a madman or liar?

John labeled the rejection of Jesus' deity as the "spirit of anti-Christ." He refused to permit the "Jesus-was-just-a-man" theory to be tolerated as an "alternative" Christian doctrine. An advocate of that position is simply a "liar," John bluntly wrote. John knew the truth; reportedly he was boiled in oil late in his life by the Romans for holding fast to the truth of what he had witnessed.

Yet, today there remain numerous so-called Christian seminaries throughout the world which attempt to refute Jesus' claim to deity. Quite frankly, they are apostate; they have forsaken the true faith. It is puzzling as to why they even bother with religious activities at all, given the claims of Jesus and all of the authors of the New Testament books. It cannot be said that their effort is simply a waste of time; in actuality, these "anti-Christs" are performing the work of their spiritual father, the Devil. There is nothing truly Christian about them.

But to those who keep an open mind about the subject, this is the supreme question which demands an answer. Life is all about playing the odds and making correct choices, right? If there is even .0001% chance that Jesus is who He claimed to be, isn't one's eternal destiny worth at least some investigation of this person Jesus? If there's even a small chance that Jesus is going to be our Judge someday, doesn't it merit a few hours of our time to learn what He wants us to do? Should we not spend some time trying to find out who He is and discover His character? Shouldn't we try to please Him?

Lawyers spend a lot of time trying to learn about the judges before whom they must appear in a trial or hearing, and attempt to present their cases, speak, write, dress, etc., in such a fashion as to please them, convince them and obtain a favorable result. How much more important is it that we "prepare our case" for life in a satisfactory manner for the One who will judge us at the end of our lives, who has the power to "cast body and soul into Hell?"

Jesus promises an answer to all those who study Him with an open mind. He won't hide Himself in mystery if we make an honest effort to search for Him. "Ask and it will be given to you; seek and you will find; knock and the door will be opened to you," He promised. Everyone who conducts such an investigation will discover the liberating truth, Jesus promised, and the Holy Spirit will be given to those who accept Him. God Himself will commune with those who seek Him, Jesus pledged. Quoting the prophet Joel, Peter proclaimed in his first sermon, "Everyone who calls on the name of the Lord will be saved." You can be one who finds Him; you can discover the Truth, in the person of Jesus Christ.

MYTH 2:
THERE WAS NO RESURRECTION

"You don't really believe Jesus physically arose from the dead, do you?" an old friend from my college undergrad days asked, rhetorically. "The resurrection was just a metaphor," she "explained" to me. "Jesus just remained alive in the hearts and minds of His followers after His death, don't you see?"

I had been eager to hear what she had learned in her first year in a Presbyterian seminary in the early 1980s. But this statement caught me completely off guard. I was so stunned that at first I thought she was joking. I hardly knew how to respond and, admittedly, fumbled around for words. Moreover, I was shocked that she would even want to pursue such a career, following a supposedly dead, powerless leader.

But since then I've discovered that a surprising number of so-called Christians join nonbelievers in the outright rejection of this second doctrine central to Christianity: that Jesus literally, bodily, physically, arose from the dead.

The proposition that Jesus was victorious over physical death is the main proof of His Godhood. So this miracle, too, must be carefully examined by nonbelievers and Christians alike to determine whether it truly occurred.

For if there were no resurrection, Christianity is a sham, a false religion based on a lie. It would not be worth living for, and certainly not worth dying for. If Jesus is still dead, the Apostle Paul writes in I Corinthians 15, then the apostles were liars; their preaching was useless. Christian faith would be empty, worthless, and hopeless. Christians would remain lost, and there would be no hope that any of us would ever be resurrected.

WOULD IT STAND UP IN COURT?

Fortunately or unfortunately, modern society settles most of its factual disputes in litigation. So would this allegation — that Jesus of Nazareth died, yet returned to life three days later — stand up in a court of law? Would the evidence supporting His resurrection be substantial enough to meet Christianity's burden of proof? Might Christians prove their case "by a preponderance of the evidence," as is required in civil litigation? Could it even be proven "beyond a reasonable doubt," the burden required in a criminal trial?

Imagine, if you will then, a court room in Jerusalem, circa 33 A.D., at which lawyers for both sides of this argument could present their evidence from both a pro and con perspective.

WHAT WOULD WITNESSES OFFER?

Hundreds of witnesses, mentioned in the four Gospels, could readily verify that Jesus actually died and that His body was sealed in a tomb for three days. They could testify that hundreds of people subsequently saw Him, heard Him speak, some even touching His wounds and dining with Him in His resurrected state. Although one might assume that Jesus' resurrection must simply be accepted by faith alone, it might be surprising just how heavy the weight of cumulative evidence favors establishing that proposition as fact.

WHAT HAD JESUS PREDICTED?

First called to the witness stand, however, might be those who heard Jesus Himself promise that He would die but not remain in the grave. Admittedly, His public pronouncements on the subject had been somewhat veiled, leaving interpretation to the individual hearer. For example, Jesus promised the "wicked generation" of His day provision of no supernatural sign except "the sign of Jonah." (Jonah had spent three days "buried" in a large sea creature and was then coughed up onto the beach, just as Jesus was to be buried in the earth for three days prior to His resurrection.) And, referring to His own body, Jesus told the Jewish leadership, "Destroy this temple, and I will raise it again in three days." Of course, some of those listeners thought that He was referring to the literal Temple in Jerusalem which had taken 46 years to build, and later used His statement against Him at His trial for sedition before the Sanhedrin.

But with the twelve disciples, Jesus was less ambiguous. They could testify that, while gathered in Galilee, He had told them that He would be "betrayed into the hands of men" who would kill Him, but "on the third day He will be raised to life." On their last trip to Jerusalem, He had told them specifically that He would be betrayed (by Judas) to the Jewish leadership, be condemned to death, turned over to the Gentiles (the Romans) to be mocked, insulted, spit upon, flogged, crucified, killed and "on the third day...raised to life" again. The disciples would explain that this direct prediction was not understood even by them until after it was fulfilled.

WAS HE REALLY DEAD?

Next, a lawyer might call to the stand the Roman guards who had been involved in Jesus' crucifixion, to establish that He definitely did die on the cross and was not entombed alive, perhaps while comatose or in some type of trance, to be "awakened" later in the cool, dark tomb, as some scoffers have accused.

Those guards would testify that His flogging alone, which lacerated chunks of flesh from His back and buttocks, could have killed a weaker man. Although likely in great physical condition, Jesus had collapsed under the weight of the cross He had been forced to drag through the street; He was already in a weakened condition after being whipped so violently and having prayed Himself to exhaustion the night before. Perhaps He was already in shock.

They would then testify that His body clearly appeared to be dead, after hanging on the cross, bleeding, with spikes driven through His extremities. They would explain that most victims of crucifixion suffocated after they became too exhausted to continue raising themselves up and down in order to breathe. But just to make certain that He was dead, one of the soldiers would testify that he had pierced the side of Jesus' trunk with a spear, erupting a sudden flow of blood and water. (He'd probably struck the pericardium, the fluid-filled sack surrounding the heart.)

They likely would explain to the jury how they, seasoned Roman executioners, had crucified hundreds of men; they knew a dead body when they saw one. They knew how to effectuate death to one who was surviving a crucifixion. They would testify as to the penalty they would suffer by their Roman superiors if the death sentence had not been fully carried out. They were personally responsible for assuring that each of the crucified victims was dead before his body was removed from the cross; the death sentence would not otherwise have been satisfied. That was their job.

Yes, they would testify, they were quite certain that Jesus was dead by the time His body was removed from the cross. There was no doubt it was a lifeless corpse.

You might also hear from expert witnesses — a physician or two. Those doctors might be asked, "Could this Man — who had been scourged, bleeding, exhausted to the point of collapse, who then had large spikes pounded through His wrists and feet, who hung on a cross for hours, continued to bleed, became severely dehydrated, and who then finally had a Roman spear punctured deeply into His side, causing the body to drain water and blood — could He have survived to the point of being able to walk around, talk, even eat within three days?"

Then, "Could that Man have only appeared to have been dead, but have remained in some type of comatose or catatonic state, still alive after suffering all of that torture?"

Unlikely, no physician could respond affirmatively to either of those questions. But even if they answered, "Improbable, but it may be possible," as physicians are fond of saying, there would be one more question. "Would this Man have been physically capable of removing a large stone that sealed His grave and overpowering several guards to escape?" It is difficult to imagine any witness responding affirmatively to that question. The stone likely weighed a ton or more.

HUNDREDS SAW HIM IN RISEN FORM

The most dramatic evidence, however, would be saved for last. Testimony of dozens, perhaps hundreds, of witnesses would swear that they saw the risen Jesus, which confirmed to them that He was not a mere mortal, but that He had overcome death itself.

They would present this testimony, knowing that it likely would cause them to be ostracized from their families and friends, thrown out of the synagogues they had always attended faithfully since birth, causing them to lose their jobs, businesses, possibly their freedom, homes, or even their lives. They'd remember that Jesus even promised such persecution for those who followed Him and believed in Him. It would be far, far easier, far better in the short term, for them to remain silent about the things they saw with their own eyes, heard with their own ears, and touched with their own fingers.

But they had to tell it, to anyone who would listen. No doubt the Spirit of God was prompting them to do so. So, one by one, they would come to the witness stand, happy and enthused to report this incredible news.

Mary, the mother of Jesus, and Mary Magdalene would be first to tell that they came to Jesus' tomb and saw with their own eyes an angel roll the sealed stone away from the tomb's entrance. The guards who'd been posted there, they would explain, were so frightened by the angel that "they shook and became like dead men." The angel then invited them into the tomb, the Marys would add, to show them that Jesus' body was no longer there. Then, while on their way, hurrying to tell the others this astonishing news, they were intercepted by none other than the risen Jesus, who told them not to fear, but to go tell His brothers to meet Him at a mountain in Galilee.

The eleven remaining disciples would testify that they initially refused to believe these two women's incredible story. Peter would tell how he ran to the tomb to check it out for himself, finding there only the linen strips which had formerly wrapped Jesus' body.

Cleopas and another follower of Jesus would tell how, on that same day, they were walking on the seven-mile road from Jerusalem to Emmaus, when a man was suddenly walking along with them, explaining prophecies about His crucifixion. When they arrived at Emmaus in the early evening, He actually had dinner with them but then disappeared as soon as they recognized His face as that of Jesus.

As Cleopas and the other follower rushed back to Jerusalem to tell the disciples about this shocking experience, Jesus suddenly appeared in the room with all of them, too. He ate fish with them and gave them further instructions.

Thomas, not present for that appearance, refused to believe such an incredible story. Perhaps he thought their grief had caused delusion or wishful thinking. So when they were assembled in the same room a week later, Jesus again appeared and instructed Thomas to touch His wounds with his own hands to prove to him that there was a physical resurrection, and that He was not a mere apparition.

Peter, James, John, Thomas and Nathanael would testify that, on a subsequent morning when they were fishing, Jesus was on the beach awaiting them as they brought their boat back to shore. And then He sat, eating fish and bread at breakfast with them. He was not a ghost or an illusion.

The eleven would explain that there were about 40 days of such appearances by the risen Jesus; and on one occasion He appeared to as many as 500 people at one time. Then, near Bethany, Jesus gave them final instructions, blessed them one last time, and then ascended into the clouds.

A STAR WITNESS

That is all well and good, you may say. All of those supposed witnesses wanted to save Jesus' reputation and fulfill His prophecy that He would arise from the dead, so they lied. Or maybe they just imagined that they saw Him. Perhaps it was even mass hypnosis of some sort.

How about presenting an unbiased witness, someone who had not been Jesus' follower during His ministry? Possibly even an enemy. We might believe someone who had no agenda or self-serving motive, right? Were there any of those available?

Funny you should ask! One final witness might be particularly credible to a First Century Jerusalem jury — a faultless keeper of the Mosaic Law, a zealous Pharisee, a "Hebrew of Hebrews" — Saul of Tarsus, to later be renamed "Paul the Apostle." Paul would testify how he had despised Christians, to the point of raging from town to town, arresting them and helping the Jewish establishment eradicate these dangerous heretics from the earth.

But much to his shock, Jesus, whose flock he had been killing, visually appeared to him and spoke audibly to Paul while he and his troops were on their way to Damascus, Syria. This frightening and totally unexpected event, which occurred weeks after the Ascension, immediately convinced Saul to become a Christian, he would explain. More incredible, he might add, Jesus actually called him to be an apostle to the despised Gentiles, the last thing this purist, Jewish zealot would have imagined or desired for his own life.

HOW STRONG THE REBUTTAL?

With that presentation completed, the "pro-resurrection" side would likely have rested its case, since the Gospels offer no other proof. But how would their opponents respond? How would they prove a "negative," i.e., that something so wonderfully strange did not occur? After all, there was a now-unsealed, empty tomb which demanded some type of explanation to the public.

The day after Jesus' body had been sealed in a new tomb, which had been donated by the wealthy Joseph of Arimathea, the chief priests and the Pharisees had requested from Governor Pilate a set of guards for the tomb, to prevent a body-snatching. It is not specified whether Pilate assigned the posting of a Sanhedrin or Roman guard, but a government seal, nevertheless, was placed on the stone at his instruction, making it illegal for any unauthorized person to remove the stone or to enter without the permission of those guards.

Upon learning from those guards that an angel had removed the stone and that the tomb was empty, the frantic Chief Priest scrambled to establish some type of "cover-up." The last thing the Jewish Establishment wanted was for the news to spread that this Jesus guy really did arise from the dead, just as He had predicted. So they reportedly bribed the tomb's guards to falsely say that Jesus' disciples had stolen His body while they, the guards, were sleeping.

So those guards would undoubtedly be the "star witnesses" to present an alternative version of events, in rebuttal to the parade of witnesses heard before.

But could they and others who denied a resurrection withstand cross-examination? As a lawyer in this case, one could have posed several questions to them, eager to hear and observe their responses:

> - *How were strong, vigilant, armed guards like themselves overpowered by Jesus' small band of non-warrior followers (so cowardly, they'd fled and scattered when He was arrested), and why hadn't anyone heard about such a newsworthy rebellion against authority?*
> - *Why hadn't these guards suffered severe criminal penalty, even death, for allowing this body-snatching to occur? Or for sleeping while on guard duty?*
> - *If they were sleeping, how could they be sure what happened?*
> - *Why were the body-snatchers not investigated, pursued, arrested and severely punished?*
> - *To where did Jesus' followers remove the body?*
> - *Why can't the body be located, to this day?*
> - *Why was the burial shroud left behind, if they smuggled away the body?*
> - *Why did these people, so fearful, timid and weak, suddenly become so emboldened that they would risk their very lives to steal a dead body?*
> - *Why were these people still proclaiming Jesus' resurrection, at risk of loss of income and reputation?*
> - *Most of the disciples had returned to their fishing nets prior to the resurrection; what would have caused this change of attitude (a sudden return to preaching) if they knew the resurrection story was fictitious?*
> - *Why do you suppose they were claiming to have seen a risen Jesus, thereby assuring that they would be expelled from the synagogues, the security of their culture, nationality and religion, of which they had been members since birth?*

To these and other questions, I suspect the responses would

have consisted of lots of "hemming and hawing," maybe even silence. What could they say?

And to this day, the doubters have never answered these questions. It is likely that an open-minded jury, having heard both sides, would have concluded that there *was* a physical resurrection of Jesus, as the prophets had foretold and as Jesus Himself had predicted.

CONTEMPORANEOUS, SECULAR REPORT

Josephus, a secular historian of that day, no Christian himself, reported the resurrection of Jesus as *fact*, "for He appeared to them alive the third day, as the divine prophets had foretold..." Apparently, even many non-Christians were convinced that there had been a resurrection. Some skeptics have questioned Josephus' quotation, noting that it had been handed down by Christian sources throughout the centuries and was therefore suspect. But even an Arabic version provides a similar quote:

> *At this time there was a wise man who was called Jesus. And his conduct was good, and he was known to be virtuous. And many people from among the Jews and other nations became his disciples. Pilate condemned him to be crucified and to die. And those who had become his disciples did not abandon his discipleship. They reported that he had appeared to them after his crucifixion and that he was alive; accordingly, he was perhaps the Messiah concerning whom the prophets have recounted wonders.*

SIGNIFICANCE OF THE RESURRECTION

If Jesus did physically arise from the dead, as He had promised, then does that not confirm that He was more than just a mere mortal? Doesn't it suggest that He was and is deity, as He professed? Does it not call for our response?

But many to this day remain too proud to accept that something extraordinary, something supernatural, probably happened circa April 33 A.D. They cling to the fragile position that there was no physical resurrection. Perhaps it was just mass delusion, hypnosis, silly superstition, fable, overactive imaginations, wishful thinking on the part of Jesus' followers, some say. They won't accept that anything supernatural has ever occurred. But most of these nonbelievers just try to ignore the issue, trying not to think about it at all.

For, you see, if one does believe in this resurrection stuff, then one might have to accept what Jesus preached: about sin, a need for a Savior, and the necessity of following His commandments. And doing that might be unpleasant; it would probably be humbling; it might be difficult. It might even disrupt a comfortable lifestyle.

Twenty-one centuries later, it still requires faith to accept this story, which admittedly does sometimes sound like a fairy tale. When even Thomas, a devotee who had been with Jesus about three years and had witnessed His miracles, had difficulty believing the good news of His resurrection, Jesus knew others would also have trouble accepting that such an unprecedented miracle occurred, especially those of us who would hear the story hundreds of years later. "[B]lessed are those who have not seen and yet have believed," He said, knowing that it would take supernatural faith to accept it.

But even logic alone strongly suggests that these hundreds of witnesses were not deluded, they were not crazy, and they were not propagating a myth due to some ulterior motive. There really is no merit to the accusation that they fabricated the Gospel story. And it was precisely because the resurrection was true that Christianity spread so rapidly, like wildfire, throughout the Roman Empire and beyond, despite the most intense persecution ever known to any fledgling religious group. Despite death, torture, and poverty and incredible persecution, the growth of the

Church was explosive. Unlike other religions, it was not spread at the point of the sword.

The resurrection of Jesus Christ can be believed today, without the requirement that one set aside his intellect, his logic and reasoning power. The facts supporting such an amazing story are credible and have never been rebutted.

He is alive today — and we can either deal with Him now, or be forced to deal with Him in the next life, at the Last Judgment at which He will preside, where *every* knee shall bow, and *every* tongue shall confess, that Jesus Christ is Lord.

MYTH 3:
JESUS' MISSION WAS
TO BE A TEACHER

Another myth or misunderstanding about Christianity is the purpose of Jesus' time on earth. Many believe that He simply was a moral teacher, providing opinions as to what God expects of us. And indeed, He did come in part to teach, even calling Himself the "light of the world." He exuded wisdom, understanding and authority like none before or since.

But while teaching, preaching and overseeing His disciples' training exercises were part of His mission, it may surprise some people to learn that education was not His primary purpose.

In short, Jesus was born to die. God was sending part of Himself (His Son) to be the perfect sacrifice for sin, so that those who believe in that Son can have a restored, perfect relationship with Him, be rescued from an eternal Hell, and are enabled to receive and enjoy eternal life. Throughout the history of His dealing with humankind, you will note that God makes demands and has requirements, but also always provides the *means* by which we can satisfy those commands. His Son is the uncomplicated method of reconciliation with Himself that He graciously provides to us.

BLOOD SACRIFICE

The concept of presenting a sacrifice to please God was not a new one to the Jews. Since what was known as Adam's fall, God demanded a sacrifice for sin — specifically, a *sinless, blood* sacrifice. To illustrate to humankind the sacrifice Jesus would make by giving His own body, God demanded that an unblemished animal die as symbolic payment for sin (because animals cannot distinguish right from wrong in the sense that humans do, they are sinless). "Without the shedding of blood there is no forgiveness," the author of Hebrews would write, remembering Moses' explanation that "it is the blood that makes atonement for one's life."

Many modern churches have removed all mention of blood sacrifice from their songs, sermons and liturgy, as something savage, barbaric and unnecessary. It's too old-fashioned and "messy" for modern Christianity, they think.

But God still demands it; "He changeth not." We are not told why God demands a blood sacrifice; He has never explained the reason. It is simply part of His sovereign plan. Perhaps it is to symbolize the concept of "a life for a life."

From the time of the first breach of His law, God had taught Adam and Eve this sacrificial concept. After eating the forbidden fruit, they had tried to cover their sin/nakedness with fig leaves but, instead, God Himself made their covering from animal skins. Just as He would later provide His Son to cover our sin with Jesus' righteousness, He killed animals and provided their garments from animal hides.

Likewise, God accepted Abel's animal offerings, but rejected Cain's grain offerings. The specific *blood* sacrifice requirement was of utmost importance to God. He saw the need to preserve and protect the purity of the blood sacrifice concept, even though His disapproval resulted in Cain murdering his brother.

Again, illustrating what He would offer by sending His own Son for a sacrifice, God provided Abraham with a ram to sacrifice as a burnt offering to Himself upon an altar, as a substitution for sacrifice of his son, Isaac. When Isaac asked his father where the sacrificial offering was, he didn't respond, "You are it!" Instead, Abraham prophetically told his son that God would provide the sacrifice. He did — and He still does. The ultimate fulfillment of the need for this sinless, perfect, blood sacrifice would be met by the substitutionary Lamb of God, the Messiah, Jesus of Nazareth.

Following in this traditional requirement which God demanded, animal sacrifice was required under the Mosaic Law, and the priests in Herod's Temple provided that service for the Jewish people for hundreds of years until their place of worship and sacrifice was destroyed by the armies of Titus, circa 70 A.D.

On the annual "Day of Atonement," Aaron was instructed to take two male goats and a ram for a burnt offering. One of the goats was to be slaughtered "for the sin offering for the people" and its blood, plus a bull's blood, placed upon the altar. Over the remaining live goat the priest was to confess "all the wickedness and rebellion of the Israelites." All of their sin for the next year was symbolically "put...on the goat's head." Then the live goat was to be released as a "scapegoat" into the desert, symbolic of the removal of the sins of the people from God's sight for another year.

JESUS' SACRIFICE PROPHESIED

So exactly how does Jesus fit into this blood sacrifice tradition and requirement?

Four hundred years before Jesus, the Prophet Isaiah had predicted that the purpose of the coming Messiah *would be to die*. More specifically, the Messiah would be the substitutionary, sacrificial Lamb of all times, dying to pay for our sins and to restore our relationship to God, to reconcile us to Him. In one of the most poetic prophecies in the Bible relating to Jesus, Isaiah wrote of him:

He grew up before him like a tender shoot,

and like a root out of dry ground.
He had no beauty or majesty to attract us to him,
nothing in his appearance that we should desire
him.

He was despised and rejected by men,
a man of sorrows, and familiar with suffering.
Like one from whom men hide their faces
he was despised, and we esteemed him not.
Surely he took up our infirmities and carried our
sorrows, yet we considered him stricken by God,
smitten by him, and afflicted.

But he was pierced for our transgressions,
he was crushed for our iniquities;
The punishment that brought us peace was upon
him, and by his wounds we are healed.
We all, like sheep, have gone astray,
each of us has turned to his own way;
and the Lord has laid on him the iniquity of us all.
He was oppressed and afflicted, yet he did not open
his mouth; he was led like a lamb to the slaughter,
and as a sheep before her shearers is silent,
so he did not open his mouth.

By oppression and judgment he was taken away.
And who can speak of his descendants?
For he was cut off from the land of the living;
for the transgression of my people he was stricken.

He was assigned a grave with the wicked, and with
the rich in his death though he had done no violence,

nor was any deceit in his mouth. Yet it was the Lord's will to crush him and cause him to suffer, and though the Lord makes his life a guilt offering, he will see his offspring and prolong his days, and the will of the Lord will prosper in his hand.

After the suffering of his soul, he will see the light of life and be satisfied; by his knowledge my righteous servant will justify many, and he will bear their iniquities.

Therefore I will give him a portion among the great, and he will divide the spoils with the strong, because he poured out his life unto death, and was numbered with the transgressors.
For he bore the sin of many, and made intercession for the transgressors.

Then, four centuries later, when the angel appeared to Joseph to tell him that Mary had conceived a Child from the Holy Spirit and that they should name Him Jesus, that heavenly messenger also explained the purpose of the Baby, consistent with the meaning of the name He was to be given: "because He will save His people from their sins."

Zechariah, the father of John the Baptist, prophesied that Jesus had come for the purpose of redeeming His people, to provide salvation.

And when the angels appeared to the Bethlehem shepherds, they gave a similar message: this Baby Jesus, whom they were to seek, would be a *Savior*.

And the prophecies continued. A devout and righteous old resident of Jerusalem, Simeon took Jesus in his arms on the day Mary and Joseph brought Him to the Temple for the ritual of circumcision. He proclaimed the Baby to be the One who would bring God's salvation. The 84-year-old prophetess Anna also confirmed to them on that day that their Son would *redeem* Jerusalem.

Without realizing it, Caiaphas, the High Priest who would condemn Jesus to death, unknowingly would also be inspired by God to proclaim Jesus' purpose, stating that it "is better for you that one Man die for the people than that the whole nation perish."

But the last "prophet," if you will, to proclaim the purpose of Jesus' visitation on earth was John the Baptist. Although John actually had been born a few months prior to Jesus, he acknowledged Jesus' deity by stating that "He was before me." Priests and Levites had been sent by the Jewish leaders to him in Bethany to ascertain whether John himself was the Messiah or the Prophet Elijah, and to determine by whose authority (*they* hadn't authorized it) John was baptizing thousands of people. John represented himself to be a fulfillment of Isaiah 40:3, and then spoke of One among them whose shoestrings he was unworthy of untying. The very next day, John identified that One as Jesus. When Jesus came down to the Jordan River to be baptized, John proclaimed, "Look, the Lamb of God who takes away the sin of the world!" He testified that Jesus is the Son of God and that He, unlike John, would "baptize [believers] with the Holy Spirit," not by water. John had the privilege of advertising to the people of Israel the purpose of Jesus' coming: that Jesus was to be the sacrificial Lamb for their sins.

JESUS EXPLAINED HIS PURPOSE

During His earthly ministry, Jesus Himself also very clearly announced the purpose for His coming. He told His disciples that His purpose was to "serve, and to give His own life as a ransom for many," and that He came to "save the world through [Himself]." In what is possibly His best-known quotation, John 3:16, Jesus explained why He was sent. "For God so loved the world that He gave His only begotten Son, that whoever believes in Him shall not perish but have eternal life." He planned to willingly surrender His life as a sacrifice for the sins of those who would believe in Him. For, you see, if Jesus had wished to resist being put to death by the Romans and Jews, He explained that He easily could have called upon 10,000 angels to protect Him. But no, Jesus compared Himself to a "good shepherd" who *voluntarily* "lays down His life for the sheep." The Father and Son *chose* this method.

Explaining to Pilate that His kingdom was not of this world, Jesus did not even oppose being executed nor did He speak in His own defense, although innocent of any crime. He willingly gave His own life to facilitate the rescue and redemption of millions of brothers and sisters, who would join Him in the coming Kingdom. Jesus compared Himself to a kernel of wheat which falls to the ground and dies, producing many seeds. (Proving he's not so brilliant, Satan orchestrated the murder of Jesus but, by doing so, assured that millions would not join him in the lake of fire! His evil "scheme" backfired on him!)

FULFILL THE LAW

Jesus also made it clear that the once-for-all-time sacrifice which He would make on behalf of mankind would fulfill the law of God. Jesus was constantly pointing out to His listeners that it was impossible for a person to fully keep the Law, to always live righteously before God. But, through His death on the cross, and our acceptance of Him as our Savior and Lord, we clothe ourselves in His perfect holiness in the eyes of God, satisfying His law. Thus, Jesus becomes our righteousness, as Jeremiah prophecied He would do.

HE BECAME OUR SCAPEGOAT

As John and Paul phrased it, Jesus became the propitiation for our sins. The substitutionary, sacrificial death of this holy, perfect Man, the unblemished Lamb, *satisfied* God's sentence of death, removing His wrath from those sinners who believe upon His

Son. Paul would write, "Therefore, there is no condemnation for one who believes in Christ." That believer has already "crossed over from death to life," Jesus assured us, and will *never* be condemned. He completed the "work" for us. The only "work" required of us is to "believe in the One He has sent," Jesus explained.

Jesus also promised that He would advocate with God the Father on behalf of those who believed in Him. He serves as our lawyer, continually reminding the Judge that our sins have been paid for by His own sacrifice; they are covered by His blood. "Whoever acknowledges Me before men, I will also acknowledge him before My Father in Heaven. But whoever disowns Me before men, I will disown him before My Father in Heaven," He cautioned, adding, "He who receives Me receives the One [God] who sent Me."

In Remembrance of Me

Before he was crucified, Jesus initiated the Church's rite of communion, sharing bread with His disciples to remind us that He gave His physical body as a sacrifice, and with them drank wine, to commemorate His "blood of the covenant, which is poured out for the forgiveness of sins."

"Do this in remembrance of Me," He requested. By this 2000-year-old, uninterrupted custom, the Church is continually reminded of *why* Jesus came, *why* He died, and *why* we are grateful and forever indebted to Him.

It Is Complete

John reports that, just before He died, Jesus cried out, "It is finished." Undoubtedly, the observers who heard those words incorrectly concluded that He was making a pronouncement about the end of His life or His ministry. Perhaps they thought He was even mourning a disastrous conclusion. But He actually made one of the most profound statements ever proclaimed by anyone. In that three-word sentence, Jesus was announcing that His purpose, His all-important mission, had been *fulfilled*. The death of this perfect, sinless God-Man satisfied and completed God's righteous demand for a sacrifice, once and for all. It satisfied the sin debt for all those who would put their complete faith in Him. *God's wrath will never be poured out upon those who accept His Son.*

As Paul would later write, quoting Deuteronomy 27:26, "Cursed is everyone who does not continue to do everything written in the [Mosaic law]." Paul also quoted Deuteronomy 21:23, "Cursed is everyone who is hung on a tree." Pointing out that none of us can ever keep God's law perfectly, Paul explained Jesus' purpose and what was accomplished by His death: Jesus took our *curse* of death by hanging on a tree and thereby redeemed us from the curse of failing to keep God's set of laws. "No one is justified before God by the Law," Paul explained to the Galatians. None of us can remain righteous an entire day, much less for a lifetime. Our evil and lustful thoughts, alone, keep us from perfection, as Jesus explained.

Quoting Habakkuk 2:4, Paul pointed to the only formula for salvation: "The righteous will live by faith." Just as Abraham's belief in God was credited as righteousness, our faith in Christ allows us to "receive the promise of the Spirit." *Jesus becomes our righteousness.*

Because Jesus' work on the cross satisfied our sin debt 100%, we can contribute nothing to the equation. It's not "50% us, 50% God," for example, or even "5% us, 95% Him," as some suppose. Our right relationship with God was earned, in its entirety, by Jesus' work. Through His Son, we can have eternal life as a *gift* from God.

NOT BY WORKS

Thus, true Christianity is the world's only religion that does not require a person to "work his way to Heaven," by doing good deeds and abstaining from evil ones.

Fear of death and doubt about the future are removed for those who believe in Christ. We don't have to worry about whether we have performed enough good deeds to outweigh the bad ones, for example. We can be eternally secure in Him from the moment we fully accept God's gift of salvation, yielding to His will, being cloaked in Jesus' righteousness, covered under His blood sacrifice. The Father who controls our eternal future declares us "not guilty," because of what Jesus did for us.

And, ironically, that life in Christ frees us from the chains of sin. For the first time, we can live holy lives by means of plugging into the power of the Holy Spirit now living within us. We, in turn, can surrender our own bodies, our lives, as *"living sacrifices, holy and pleasing to God."*

During the last three hours of Jesus' human life, the thick veil hanging in the Temple which kept all but the elite priests out of God's holy presence, split apart from the top to the bottom, supernaturally torn open. God's salvation plan was now *opened to all*, without danger, mystery, fear, or need of animal sacrifice. He no longer presented His Spirit only in that Temple. Jews and Gentiles alike, through God's Son, could be justified. The priests, the rituals, the sacrifices, were no longer required under this New Covenant which God had made with humankind.

And, within about 35 years of Jesus' death, the Temple itself would be destroyed. Since its destruction, circa 70 A.D. by the Romans, the Jews have had nowhere to offer the sacrifices prescribed by Moses for sin offering. Instead, God has provided a perfect, for all times, sacrifice in his Son, giving us a choice to accept or reject Him. The bodies of the believers are His current temples; the Holy Spirit dwells within them, not in buildings or boxes like the Ark of the Covenant.

NO OTHER SACRIFICE

So if we continue to reject that one-time, perfect, blood sacrifice Jesus has made on our behalf, "no [other] sacrifice for sins is left, but only a fearful expectation of judgment and of raging fire that will consume the enemies of God," the Bible tells us.

Unless we accept His Son, our sin debt remains uncovered, and we are spiritually naked, subjecting us to God's wrath. We are walking dead men and women, already judged. As He had proclaimed, only Jesus is *the* Way, *the* Truth, and *the* Life, and no one can come to the Father except through Him. Without this protective "skin" God has prepared and provided for me through His Son's death on the cross, I continue to be His rebellious enemy, subject to an eternal punishment which separates me from Him and all that is good. I certainly can't live with Him throughout eternity in that rebellious, unreconciled state.

Thus, the millions who through the centuries have physically tortured themselves, who have lived with guilt, who have made numerous sacrifices and gifts to their gods, who have even given their lives, attempting to work their way toward God's approval, have done so in vain. Faith in Jesus Christ is all that they have ever needed to become right with God.

As awesome and complex as His sacrifice was, Jesus made acceptance of Him an extremely easy proposition. It is so simple that even a small child's prayer, a question from a dying criminal on the cross beside him, the cry of a soldier on a battlefield or the soft, even unspoken, plea of a patient in a hospital bed, is heard.

And God's response is always positive; there are no rejections to those who sincerely and honestly seek Him. To all who receive Christ, who believe in His name, is given "the right to become children of God."

MYTH 4:
THE CHURCH IS FULL OF HYPOCRITES

"I might attend church if there just weren't so many hypocrites."

How often have Christians heard that response? It may be the most popular objection nonbelievers raise against Christianity. It's the "I'm-just-as-good-as-they-are" excuse.

But these critics are themselves being a bit hypocritical. It doesn't matter to them that there are hypocrites in politics, among film and sport stars, teachers, even friends and the people they date. They don't give up on them. But somehow, people are eager to abandon a pursuit of Christ because there are phonies in the Church. It's the biggest excuse in the book!

WE'VE ALL SEEN THEM

No question, there are quite a few hypocrites in the Church and there always have been. It's not only the high-profile TV evangelists caught in corruption, sexual sins and greed, or the predatory, pedophile priests who add to the skepticism of the public by leading a double life. We've all observed many fakes in religious circles, unfortunately. The gossiping troublemaker, who sits on the front pew. The church treasurer stealing from offering plates. The philanthropist who sits as a director of religious organizations but who makes his millions by cheating customers, mistreating employees and taking unfair advantage of his competitors. The church leader with an addiction. Or even "do-as-I-say-not-as-I-do" parents.

True, born-again Christians should constantly examine their lives to question whether there is any sin or hypocrisy and, if so, confess it to God, repent of it immediately, then flee from any temptation or evil.

I later discovered that the evangelist preaching at the service at which I first became a believer was conducting an adulterous affair at the time! (It's amazing the amount of good that can occur as the result of ministries headed by hypocritical, even very sinful, individuals. But if God can use a donkey to speak the truth to Balaam, it's no problem for Him to use a "fallen" preacher to effectively deliver the Gospel to receptive hearts. The message remains pure and effective even if the messenger is not.)

Indeed, there are very few Christians who have not acted hypocritically at least once in a while. It is a problem in the Church; we can't deny that.

Jesus frequently spoke out against hypocrisy, especially among the Jewish religious leaders who imposed their strict, demanding and harsh legalism upon their people but who possessed corrupt, proud, judgmental and greedy hearts themselves. Using a carpentry metaphor, He cautioned against complaining about "the speck of sawdust in your brother's eye" when you have "a plank in your own eye."

The Scribes and Pharisees followed not only the Law of Moses, but also all the thousands of rules and traditions that had developed since the law was given. They were so legalistic that they wouldn't pick up a coin on the Sabbath, because it was considered work. They expected, and were given, great honor by the people of Israel in that day. One of the sayings of that time was, "If only two people get into Heaven, one will be a Scribe and the other a Pharisee." From the outside, it appeared to the people of

Jesus' day that they were pleasing God like none other.

So think how shocked the audience must have been when, in the middle of the Sermon on the Mount, Jesus suddenly said, "For I tell you that unless your righteousness surpasses that of the Pharisees and the teachers of the law [Scribes], you will certainly not enter the Kingdom of Heaven." That statement must have awakened those who were nodding off! How could anyone possibly be saved if you had to do better than the Scribes and Pharisees? Weren't they as good as it got? Who could be more righteous?

But Jesus called those sects "snakes and vipers"! Unlike the other people, He saw inside their hearts. He knew that the thoughts and motives of the Pharisees and Scribes were just as evil, as corrupt, as any other sinner. Actually it was worse because they were pretending to be something they weren't and were also imposing a heavy burden of rules upon the people. Jesus said they were "like whitewashed tombs, which look beautiful on the outside but on the inside are full of dead men's bones and everything unclean," adding, "In the same way, on the outside you appear to people as righteous but on the inside you are full of hypocrisy and wickedness. Woe to you, teachers of the law and Pharisees, you hypocrites!" They strained at gnats but swallowed camels, He said. Jesus noted how they tithed down to even offering a tenth of the mint, cumin and dill they'd grown, but ignored the more important requirements of God, like justice, mercy, and faithfulness. They were dirty cups which needed to be cleaned inside, He said. (Can you see why Jesus was so popular with the religious rulers of His day?)

So Jesus made it clear that God is highly, intensely offended by those who pretend to be holy but are not. It's far better to admit we are sinners.

THEY'RE NOT ALL CHRISTIANS!

Knowing all about hypocrisy, Jesus predicted that many who claimed to be His followers would not be genuine. "Many are invited but few are chosen," He would say.

Illustrating that fact, one of His parables told of a farmer sowing seeds. Seeds which the planter dropped on the path were snatched away and eaten by birds (symbolizing "the evil one"). Others, sown in shallow, rocky soil, sprouted but were scorched and withered by the sun (symbolic of those who fall away under persecution). Other seeds were choked out by thorns (symbolizing "the worries of this life" and "the deceitfulness of wealth"). But a few of the seeds fell into good soil (symbolic of those true Christians who hear the Word, understand it, and produce fruits of the Spirit in their lives), and survived and thrived.

In another parable, Jesus predicted that the enemy (Satan) would plant weeds or "tares" (fake Christians) among the wheat (true believers), which would grow together, undetectable, until harvest time (God's Judgment). Many hypocrites will *appear* to be genuine, even *great* Christians, to many of us here on earth.

Jesus calls His disciples to be "fishers of men." A professional fisherman will tell you that his nets catch not only edible fish, but also many which must be thrown back into the sea or be destroyed. So it is with those who claim to be followers of Christ.

When He returns, Jesus promises that He'll separate those who are His from those who are not, "as a shepherd separates the sheep from the goats." Those who belong to Him will inherit the Kingdom He's prepared for them since the creation of the world, but the others "will go away to eternal punishment."

In one of the most frightening passages in the Bible, Jesus implies that we will be shocked by those who make it into His Kingdom and those who do not. "Not everyone who says to Me, 'Lord, Lord,' will enter the Kingdom of Heaven, but only he who does the will of My Father who is in Heaven," Jesus warned. "Many will say to Me [because Jesus will be our final Judge] on that day, 'Lord, Lord, did we not prophesy in Your name, and in Your name drive out demons and perform many miracles?' Then I will tell them plainly, 'I never knew you. Away from Me, you evildoers!'"

So how is it that we can be part of Jesus' Kingdom? His words above tell us exactly how: by doing the Father's will (which starts by believing upon His Son) and by "knowing" Jesus Christ. But there will be many high-profile "religious" people here on earth, incorrectly thought by millions to be great saints of God, maybe even having done many wonderful works, who appeared to be Christians but never knew Jesus on the intimate, loving basis required to become a child of God.

HEROES OR HYPOCRITES?

Having said all that, we must understand that even true Christians are "not perfect, they're just forgiven," as the bumper sticker aptly puts it. The world of unbelievers too often has unreasonable, un-Biblical expectations, an ultra-high standard requiring Christians to never sin, never make mistakes, never stumble and fall. And when they do, it is unfairly charged that these Christians are hypocrites. But sometimes they are simply human beings who have imperfections. They are not pretending to be something they are not.

The Bible-illiterate might be shocked to learn about the flawed men and women who are held up as mighty heroes of the faith, given as examples to millions. Some of us undoubtedly would have "written off" many of those individuals as unsalvageable, useless to God:

> • Abraham twice lied about the identity of his
> wife to save his own skin. And refused to wait for
> God's promise of a son to him and Sarah his wife,
> instead impregnating Hagar, his Egyptian servant.
> He even had children by several concubines! Yet,
> because he "believed the Lord...He credited it to
> him as righteousness." In the highest possible
> honor, Abraham was even called "God's Friend,"
> and selected by God to father the millions of Jews,
> God's chosen people.

- King David committed adultery with a married Bathsheba. Then, after getting her pregnant, he had her husband sent to the battlefront to be killed to cover up his misdeeds. But he eventually repented of these two horrible sins, suffering terrible earthly judgment for them, including the death of their child and a costly rebellion by another son, Absalom. He had numerous wives and concubines. He slew thousands, often needlessly. Yet it was from David's lineage that the Messiah came and his throne upon which the Messiah will reign. David's Psalms may be the most popular book of the Bible. And despite his sin, the Bible calls David "a man after [God's] own heart," one whose heart was "fully devoted" to God.
- King Solomon, David's son, married many foreign wives, joining with them and turning to other gods, and God punished him for it. Yet, he was considered the wisest and wealthiest man, perhaps of all times, and was even allowed to build the first Temple. He wrote part of the Scriptures.
- There were many other flawed "heroes" of the Bible, including Sarah, Jacob, Moses (a murderer), Rahab (a harlot), Samson, Peter, James, and John, to name only a few. Peter cursed and denied Jesus three times and even "dropped out" after Jesus was crucified, but later was reconciled with his risen Lord to become the first leader of the Church, powerful, effective, and eventually, according to tradition, was himself crucified for his faith.
- And hear what Paul, perhaps the greatest (certainly the most prolific) writer of the New Testament, had to confess about himself:

We know that the law is spiritual; but I am unspiritual,

sold as a slave to sin. I do not understand what I do. For what I want to do I do not do, but what I hate I do... I know that nothing good lives in me, that is, in my sinful nature. For I have the desire to do what is good, but I cannot carry it out. For what I do is not the good I want to do; no, the evil I do not want to do — this I keep on doing... So I find this law at work: When I want to do good, evil is right there with me. For in my inner being I delight in God's law; but I see another law at work in the members of my body, waging war against the law of my mind and making me a prisoner of the law of sin at work within my members. What a wretched man I am!... So then, I myself in my mind am a slave to God's law, but in the sinful nature a slave to the law of sin.

OUR HOPE IS IN CHRIST

If these great men and women of the Bible couldn't live perfectly holy lives all of the time, then what hope is there for any of us?

Without constantly "plugging into" the power of the Holy Spirit, which every true Christian has within himself, we can do nothing to consistently lead a sinless, holy life. The reason for that is because our regenerated spirits remain housed in bodies which naturally seek pleasure and ease. We're naturally selfish. And our inseparable bodies and minds are "diseased" as the result of "Adam's fall." We may say and do things we don't want to do, simply because of shifts in our glucose or hormonal levels or blood pressure, just as examples. Moreover, we live among sinful people which makes it difficult not to be contaminated and led astray. All that, along with other temptations which can even be demonic in origin (Satan goes about as a "roaring lion looking for someone to devour," Peter writes), causes true Christians to sin from time to time. None is perfect, although perfection should be every believer's constant goal.

We are called to holiness, not happiness, I've heard a pastor say. Peter encouraged believers to make every effort to add to their faith, goodness; to goodness, knowledge; to knowledge, self-control; to self-control, perseverance; to perseverance, godliness; to godliness, brotherly kindness; and to brotherly kindness, love. (These are the stages, interestingly, through which most believers progress, sequentially, in their walk with Christ.) Those qualities will make us productive and assure ourselves and others that we are true Christians.

SUMMARY

Are there hypocrites in the Church? There surely are, perhaps millions, of nonbelievers posing as Christians. They've been there for 2000 years and will continue to be there until an all-knowing Jesus sorts them out.

Are there flawed but genuine Christians? Absolutely! All of us are imperfect, some much worse than others. With guidance by the Holy Spirit, most improve with time and experience, thankfully.

But noticing this, or misunderstanding it, is not a valid excuse for failing to heed Christ's invitation. Each of us, individually, will stand before Him some day to give an account of our *own* lives, and we cannot point to what those in Christian ministry may have done or failed to do. We can't blame our refusal to accept Him on actions or inactions of parents, spouses, co-workers, or others.

That's why each needs to accept the cloak of Jesus' holiness which is freely offered to us now. For none of us will ever be able to perform enough good deeds to outweigh our sin and our failures. We need to take on *His* righteousness by accepting His free gift of salvation. "Choose for yourselves this day whom you will serve." Jesus promises that His yoke is easy and His burden is light. He is not a harsh taskmaster.

As Jesus pointed out, in the Parable of the Wedding Banquet, we will not enter His kingdom without that cloak of righteousness which He now freely offers to us.

Myth 5:
I'd Need to Clean Up
My Life to Become a Christian

Paul tells us that the truth of God is known instinctively; God installs this awareness "software" of Himself in our minds, our consciences. In our "heart of hearts," we must admit that we were born with this knowledge. Scientists have even demonstrated, by SPECT imaging technology of the brain, that we are "hard-wired to believe in God." No one will ever have the valid excuse of claiming that he did not know that there was a God, a Creator, a moral law. I'm not aware of any ancient culture that did not worship some type of deity.

Love of the World

So why do so many people refuse to become Christians, even in Western society where the Gospel has been widely disseminated and there are few other competing religions? Why do they refuse this "no works," gracious offer by Jesus of eternal life?

Most resist, I think, because they love the things offered by this world more than they love God. Indeed, John wrote that when we love the world we show that we do not have the love of the Father in us. He continues, "For the world offers only the lust for physical pleasure, the lust for everything we see, and pride in our possessions. These are not from the Father. They are from this evil world." So in our natural state we prefer the fleeting, temporary pleasures of this life to the eternal value of surrendering all of it to Christ, and allowing Him to be our Master and Lord. To put it bluntly, we enjoy our sin, or at least think we do.

Many are unwilling to delay their short-term gratification by conforming their will to God's in hope of a heavenly reward. And others, of course, believe that this world is all there is, that we are guaranteed no afterlife, so why not do as we please?

THE DANGERS OF PRIDE

Second, people fail to come to Christ because they refuse to humble themselves. Admitting that I am a sinner, becoming a Christian, being baptized, confessing my faith to other people, living an obedient life, and conceding to God the lordship that He deserves, all require humility that I do not naturally possess or easily acquire.

Without a doubt, the most dangerous of all sin is pride. The rebellion that pride caused is what brought Lucifer (Satan) and his fellow angels crashing down. It is what keeps men and women from acknowledging that they are sinners and admitting they need a Savior, and prevents them from submitting to Christ's lordship. It is at the root of most other sinful behaviors, directly or indirectly. It has been my observation that one need not be wealthy, prominent, beautiful or brilliant to lack humility. Poor, ugly, uneducated, so-called "nobodies" of society are equally full of foolish pride.

Our culture itself promotes pride. Not only pride in our physical appearance, possessions, abilities, etc., but also the more harmful pride that says, "I'm self-sufficient; I'm self-reliant; I don't need any help from God or man." It's extremely counter-culture to be humble, wouldn't you agree?

God resists such proud people, James warns. They claim to be wise without God, becoming utter fools instead. These proud ones foolishly condemn the Gospel without understanding what it can do for them, Peter adds.

That's why Jesus revealed that we obtain entry into His Kingdom only if we *become as little children.* In other words, only if we come to Him — in humility, in need, in total dependance upon Him, accepting that His knowledge and wisdom and ways are far greater than our own — can we truly become His followers.

We must also acknowledge that all we possess — intelligence, position, family, possessions, looks, health — are gifts from God. And that is very difficult to do — impossible, actually — if we shield ourselves in a barrier of pride. We need help from the Holy Spirit's convicting power, plus some life experiences to "take us down a few notches," to even begin this journey toward becoming humble before God.

Sadly, we've seen many people stubbornly take that God-resistant pride with them to their graves. And for what? What did it prove? Whom did they impress? Did they expect that their friends and family would sit around after they're gone and remark, "One thing you can say about ol' Joe — he never gave in to any of that Jesus stuff!"? In such cases, his loved ones would more likely try to divert their thoughts at his funeral by recalling something good about ol' Joe's life, but avoid thinking too much about where his soul may now reside.

JUST AS I AM

But then there are many people who have another reason for resisting the message of Christ. They carry the misconception that they must somehow "clean up their act" and quit sinning before God will accept them. Many of these folks are sincere; they have just been misled at some point during their lives, or have misunderstood the Gospel message.

But, to the contrary, the Bible makes it clear that we are not even *capable* of cleansing ourselves from sinful thoughts and behavior in our natural, unregenerated state. And such a view demonstrates a misunderstanding of how we are saved, a misunderstanding of God's grace.

There is no reference to Jesus or His disciples ever requiring anyone to change in any way before becoming His follower. In fact, there are many opposite examples. Jesus simply called His disciples to "follow" Him. Likely, it was only later that their repentance (turning from sin) became obvious. In some cases such as Matthew, the crooked tax collector, however, the changes were swift and obvious; he immediately began refunding excessive taxes to his former victims.

The classic illustration of God's grace is given in Jesus' conversation with one of the criminals who hung on a cross next to Him. That convict probably had never done too many good deeds in his life, but undoubtedly had done a lot of evil ones. There's no record he was ever baptized or participated in any religious rite or act. Initially, he'd joined the other malefactor in taunting the Son of God. Yet, when he later softened and asked, "Jesus, remember me when You come into your kingdom," Jesus promised him that he would join Him in Paradise that very day! This wicked criminal is one of only a handful of people mentioned in the Bible whom we know to be in Heaven today.

It's a Gift!

We can't "buy our way" or "earn our way" into Heaven. If you haven't noticed, the great majority of true Christians during the past two millennia generally have been the poor, uneducated, and oppressed, as opposed to the intellectuals or rich ruling class, the latter often having been nominal Christians or nonbelievers.

This comes as no surprise to Christ, but is according to His plan. He praised God for hiding "these things from the wise and learned [the intellectuals and well-educated], and reveal[ing] them to little children." He added, "Yes, Father, for this was Your good pleasure." It would be easier for a camel to go through the eye of a needle than a rich person to get into Heaven, Jesus said. The wisdom of this world is foolishness in God's sight, Paul wrote. We may think we're so important, so smart, but God knows better; He sees through us. He knows the big picture; after all, He created it, whether we think so or not. Our little bit of knowledge and power are trivial, nothing to Him.

And it can be a shocking concept to nonbelievers who mistakenly think they must reach some level of sinlessness, do some type of penance, suffer, agonize or perform some type of work, in order to be pleasing and acceptable to God. Some refuse to accept that it can be so uncomplicated.

Others will accept that works do not save them, but incorrectly think works *keep* them saved. As Paul wrote to the Church at Ephesus, however, it is by grace through faith that we are saved, not anything we do or refrain from doing; it is rather a gift from God. Jesus' death satisfied God's requirements for those who believe in Him. "For if we could be saved by keeping the law (being good, following God's rules), then there was no need for Christ to die," Paul wrote to the Church at Galatia.

Salvation, the New Testament explains, is of God, not man's doing. The writer of Hebrews even tells us that it is God, not us, who is the "author" and " finisher" of our faith. God is the One who draws us to Himself, and He's also the One who secures our faith and assures that we will go to Heaven to be with Him when we die.

God was aware of every sin you and I were ever going to commit during our entire lifetimes, long before we were even born, before this earth even existed. Like an observer viewing a parade from a helicopter, He sees our life from beginning to end, all at one time. And when we come to Christ, accepting God's free gift of salvation, those sins — past, present and future sins — are all forgiven. We "get saved" by grace alone and we "stay saved" by grace alone. This is such a generous proposition that even many genuine Christians cannot understand or fully accept it! Someone has said, "Grace is everything for nothing, to people who don't deserve anything." This is the *"Amazing Grace"* that millions have sung about over the years.

In God's view (because of the blood sacrifice made by Jesus' death on our behalf), our sins which were "scarlet" now become "white as snow." It's as if He views us through a filter of this redeeming blood of the Lamb.

A Pig Enjoys His Mud!

Christians sometimes consider it their mission to reform the evils of the world. Indeed, some Christian-initiated crusades, such as ending slavery, finally caught on and were successful. But most of those efforts to impose Biblical morality upon the world — whether they be with regard to prohibition of alcohol, stopping abortion, preventing divorce, curbing sexual sins, reducing violence, and the like — have pretty much failed.

These well-meaning Christians forget that, unless there is repentance — a change of heart — there will be no long-term reform, either in individuals or in nations. And they forget that we aren't called to reform the world, but to proclaim Christ, the only Author of truly changed lives. "The man without the Spirit does not accept the things that come from God, for they are foolishness to him, and he cannot understand them, because they are spiritually discerned," Paul explains. Jesus said that men naturally love darkness better than light because our deeds are evil. Unless the Spirit intervenes, we don't even desire to change our lifestyle, attitude, and actions.

Becoming a New Creature

Unless one's mind and heart has been renewed and regenerated, his natural tendency is to satisfy his own lusts, pride, greed, convenience, and comfort, what the Bible calls "loving the world." But once we accept Christ as Lord and Savior, we then begin a journey in which we are "controlled not by the sinful nature but by the [Holy] Spirit" that now lives within us, Paul writes. And, he adds, anyone who belongs to Christ possesses the third member of the Trinity, the Holy Spirit. (There is no waiting period for some type of "second experience" after being saved, in which the Holy Spirit comes upon a believer, as some incorrectly teach.) This Holy Spirit who has drawn us to Christ now acts as a "Super Conscience" within us, convicting, guiding, comforting, encouraging and assuring us. And we are admonished as Christians to be filled with the Holy Spirit, to keep drinking from His fountain.

Although the work within each of them was supernatural, most Christians I know did not have some type of mystical or emotional experience when they first became believers. But they all began to view life differently, as if seeing it through God's eyes.

Paul tells us, "Therefore, if anyone is in Christ, he is a new creation; the old has gone, the new has come. All this is from God, who reconciled us to Himself through Christ and gave us the ministry of reconciliation..."

Hearts which once had been hardened toward other people now may become softer; greed and stinginess may turn to generosity and graciousness; selfishness may be replaced by service; hatred and bigotry turn into love and understanding; pride changes to humility; lust gives way to self-control and dignity; and meanness and abusiveness surrender to temperance, kindness, sympathy and helpfulness. A Christian often changes the places where he chooses to hang out, as well. He may change his attitude toward family and job, even redirecting his college or career. Sometimes he's no longer comfortable with the same set of friends, nor are they comfortable with him. Often the first noticeable change is an intense hunger to learn what God has to say, which leads him to study the Bible. And through the Spirit's help, he truly understands the Word of God for the first time in his life. By this enlightenment of the Spirit, even those Bible miracles and stories — concepts which once seemed like foolish myths and fables believed only by the feeble-minded — suddenly become reality, wisdom and truth, because he now trusts the veracity of the book's Author.

These changes, in turn, cause him to be grieved and offended by things that he did not likely even consider to be wrong when he was in his unconverted state. I changed my view on abortion as I became a mature believer, for example. A believer might even change his eating and drinking habits, or stop putting certain substances into his body, since he realizes it is now "the temple of the Holy Spirit." A Christian may feel condemned over wearing certain styles of provocative dress. Often, matters which once seemed so terribly important — politics, leisure and sporting events, literature, entertainment, social circles, climbing the corporate ladder, "keeping up with the Joneses," even world events — suddenly are recognized as temporal affairs, almost petty and insignificant compared to eternal issues and the awesome excitement of serving God. For some of us, becoming a true follower of Christ was like putting on prescription glasses after suffering from terribly blurred or darkened vision for many years.

As a result of some of these changes in our lives, we see immediate benefit and are thankful. Others, admittedly, will not be fully appreciated until later, perhaps not even understood in this lifetime.

This process is what the Bible calls "sanctification," or a "setting apart" of believers from the unconverted world. Just as God gave the Israelites kosher laws through Moses which protected and made them separate and a "peculiar people unto himself," Christ also calls His people to be a "holy nation, a peculiar people." God desires for His people to be holy, as He is holy.

But we do not — we cannot — begin that process of progressive holiness, the continual sanctification process — until *after* we surrender our lives to Christ and begin that journey.

Paul and Peter compared this refining process God performs in believers to what a goldsmith does in removing impurities from his metals. If we are His children, God disciplines, chastens and molds us to His likeness. Just as with the experience of a child being punished and corrected by earthly parents, it is not always a fun or pleasant process, however.

Observing the changes in people who've become believers

undoubtedly causes many nonbelievers to stay away. They scoff at it. As John noted, they enjoy their sin, they enjoy the temporary pleasures this world can offer, and they do not want to undergo the changes they see occurring in their former friends and family who have become Christians. Instead, they prefer the "instant gratification" offered by this world's pleasures.

SUMMARY

So God does not require anyone to clean up his act before coming to Him. He'll take care of "scrubbing us up" after we surrender our lives to Him. And, to those of us believers who sometimes think it's our job to change the world, we can keep an old saying in mind: "He calls us to be fishers of men. You catch them, He cleans them."

Oh, you don't think He can change you? Trust me, He will either do it the "easy way" — with your cooperation — or the "hard way," if you resist. He will orchestrate your circumstances for your own long-term benefit, which I know from personal experience. He makes changes in His children by a means the psychologists call "positive re-enforcement," involving rewards, satisfaction, pleasant developments which encourage us to draw closer to Him and obey His laws. But He also uses "negative re-enforcement," through disciplinary measures, hardship, setbacks and other difficulties at times, to accomplish the same goals.

God causes His followers to hate evil and to love good, conforming our lives to His way, slowly but surely, in His sanctification process. And each time we reach a higher level in our Christian walk, He urges us, spurs us on, to yet greater heights. He is constantly buffing, polishing us up.

The first step is to obey Jesus' simple request: "Follow Me." And for those of us who call ourselves Christians, we need to constantly test ourselves to make sure that we are "in the faith," Paul warns. In other words, I need to examine whether or not I'm really a Christian. Am I trying to do all the things Christ commanded, trying to please Him? "Do not merely listen to the Word, and deceive yourselves," James writes. "Do what He says." Do we have the "fruit of the Spirit," which includes love, joy, peace, patience, kindness, goodness, faithfulness, gentleness and self-control? Possession of these "good fruit" proves to ourselves, and to others, that we are truly children of God.

MYTH 6:
ALL CHURCHES ARE ALIKE

From the outside — say, for example, from the Islamic world — Christianity may appear to be a unified entity, with one history, of one thought and speaking with one voice. But those within Christendom — whether Orthodox, Catholic or Protestant — know that's far from reality. There may be 3,000 to 5,000 varieties of denominations of those who call themselves churches of Jesus Christ. It may be the most fragmented and disunified of all organized world religions.

But there is actually only one, true Christian faith. "Make every effort to keep the unity of the Spirit through the bond of peace," Paul commanded the Church at Ephesus. "There is one body and one Spirit — just as you were called to one hope when you were called — one Lord, one faith, one baptism, one God and Father of all who is over all and through all and in all." Despite what some say to the contrary, there *are* absolutes regarding correct doctrine, awaiting our discovery.

The Church was fragmented into different thoughts, different camps, from the First Century, however. There was very little unity from the outset. Much of Paul's struggles in his missionary work were against those from within (primarily the "Judaizers," who were teaching that belief in Christ alone was not enough for salvation, that keeping the Jewish law was also required). He was very adamant about keeping the purity of the Gospel message, i.e., salvation by grace alone, not by works, through faith in Christ. He was most upset by those who preached a "different gospel." This "different gospel" is "really no gospel at all," he pointed out. For emphasis, Paul twice cursed, in the strongest terms, anyone who preached any "gospel other than the one we preach to you." Paul knew how dangerous and harmful would be a fragmented doctrine which added or detracted anything from the basic Gospel message.

But those admonitions from Paul and others did not stop the deep divisions, even in the first Church. Even leaders such as Peter were initially allowing the Gospel to be augmented, unable to sever their lifelong ties to the customs and requirements of the Mosaic Law. Paul actually opposed Peter to his face for this legalism, which he characterized as hypocrisy, and which he contended was leading believers astray.

It finally required a church council, convened in Jerusalem, to resolve the fissure and conflict between the legalists and the purists. The legalists wanted Gentile Christians to be circumcised and required to obey the Law of Moses. But Peter, likely now convinced by Paul of the correctness of the opposing position, argued that, "It is through the grace of our Lord Jesus that we are saved." Even so, it appears that there was a slight compromise with the legalists, and the Church agreed to ban eating food polluted by idols, meat from strangled animals and from ingesting blood. Unity of doctrine was difficult to attain, even by the apostles.

Jesus prayed for those given to Him by the Father, "that they may be one as We are One." "May they be brought to complete unity," He asked God. Looking around today at Christianity, one might assume that Jesus' petition was denied. But, if we believe Jesus was in complete harmony with the Father, then we must assume this and all of His prayers were answered. We must assume that there has always been a unified, true Church, albeit scattered among many diverse branches and denominations. As illustrated in the Parable of the Wheat and Tares, we can safely assume that there are true Christians throughout the churches of the world, interspersed among those who merely appear to be Christians. They eventually will be sorted out by the Judge who sees their hearts; only He truly knows who belongs to Him and who does not.

CULTURAL DIVERSITY

Again, to outsiders, trying to put one single face on the Christian religion must be puzzling, even amusing.

On one end of the spectrum, you have the "high church" worship style of the Catholics, Orthodox faiths, some Episcopal and other traditional Protestants. Until recent years, at least, these churches conducted ritualistic liturgy, often ceremonial in style, dominated by the clerical hierarchy, and for centuries even conducted in Latin, using ancient music and text. The garb of the clergy and the building in which the worshipers gathered was often ornately decorated, even very costly. The style of their services tended to be very formal and somber, repetitive, varying little from week to week.

Some might consider the opposite end of the worship style spectrum to reside in the Southern white and African-American churches in the Pentecostal and Holiness tradition. In many of those churches the style is far more demonstrative. The worshipers are much freer in their participation, even swaying with their bodies, jumping, running, falling to the floor at times. They sing loud and lively songs, often with equally loud and fast music (which many historians think were the roots of rock-n-roll). They may raise their hands, cry, shout, pray aloud as a congregation, stand to give personal testimonies, even "speak in unknown tongues." A few of these churches do not allow paintings in their simple church buildings; they wouldn't even consider allowing statues of dead saints, which they would consider idolatry, a violation of the Second Commandment. Rather than being subject to a strict denominational hierarchy, these individualistic churches often stand alone with their own rules and unique doctrine, following a pastor's teaching, with little or no interference by a bishop or denominational conference, much less anything remotely like a cardinal or pope.

Another Christian variety some might view as another extreme on the spectrum was the old Quaker denomination where members would sit in silence, praying and contemplating the Word of God until "moved by the Spirit" to speak. Some of these had no formal pastor or leader at all.

While the lines between these worship styles have blurred in recent decades, and there are thousands of varieties between these opposite poles, the "high church" worshipers have often berated the opposite style as "holy rollers" and they, in turn, call them the "frozen chosen," the "dead" and other select names. Each could not imagine how the other could possibly represent the true Church.

There have been numerous restoration movements over the centuries, the most significant of which was led by Martin Luther and other Protestant reformers in the 1500s. Each reformer claims to be trying to return the Church to the true doctrines and style of worship of that Early Church. Others take great pride in "staying true" to traditions that have been handed down for hundreds of years within their denomination, even if they don't know their origin or purpose.

I was once among those who believe that there is only one basic way of worship that is pleasing to God, and that all others must surely be wrong. I suspect many Christians have shared that view at some point in their lives.

But now I can see that genuine devotion and praise of God can take many forms and perhaps many, if not all, are pleasing to Him. His creativity is infinite. Just as He created nature and the people of the world in great varieties, colors, sounds and shapes, perhaps God enjoys the wide variety of church service styles. Perhaps He's even authored and encouraged it.

I now realize that we must respect the cultural differences within the Church, accepting that there probably are true believers among its varied branches, even if we personally would never be comfortable with every other worship style.

DOCTRINAL DIFFERENCES

The difference in theology and doctrine among those who call themselves Christians, however, is a different matter. Even allowing for wide liberality for diversity of thought and equally valid interpretation of God's Word, there are teachings which are so different, so opposite, that they cannot possibly all be correct. The Ecumenical Movement, which has seen some success in recent decades, has attempted to blur, compromise, or even put aside those doctrinal differences in order to unify various Christian church organizations, but the gap between the denominations in many instances remains too wide to mend. Some are allowing the worst kinds of sin to be tolerated in their congregations and clergy.

And this, again, goes back to the "wheat and tares." Some are true Christian doctrines and some are not. God will eventually sort it all out.

But if we are to be true followers of Christ, we need to diligently seek the truth, what God requires of us, rather than blindly following the teachings of our own church organization or what our parents taught us. It's possible to do that by returning to the primary source, the recorded teachings of Jesus, His apostles and other writers of the New Testament, whom we believe were inspired by God. Christ did not call for unity at any cost; it is not to be purchased at the high price of heresy.

THREE TYPES OF CHURCHES

Despite the fact that there are thousands of denominations throughout the world today that label themselves as Christian, I think there are basically only three main types. They are separated and categorized by one difference, essentially: how they view and interpret the Bible.

APOSTATE

Many so-called Christian churches, possibly the majority, do not view the Bible as the inspired, Living Word of God. Their leaders have been taught in liberal seminaries that the Bible is merely myth, poetry or literature, containing distorted and self-serving information, perhaps some of it being of historical value. At best, they teach that the Bible represents humankind's *search* for God, search for truth, but certainly not *the* Truth. The Bible is a mix of truth and fiction, they say, like any secular collection of literature might be. Its authors were no more inspired by God than Mark Twain, they believe.

Because the Bible is discounted and not held to be the final authority or basis for doctrine for everyday living, these "churches" have ended up in many cases becoming no more than civic or political organizations. One is far more likely to hear messages about "social justice" (i.e., socialism), "tolerance of other lifestyles," "respecting other cultures," or "save the environment" propaganda coming from their pulpits, rather than anything remotely touching on a discussion of sin or the need for repentance and a Savior. As Paul prophesied, this End Times "church" worships the creation, not the Creator. In fact, these so-called churches are far more likely to talk about evolution than God's creation. Lower life forms, over which God gave man dominion, are esteemed as highly as human beings, often higher than unborn human beings.

Many of these churches, which once possessed sound doctrine and were on fire for God, mostly mainstream Protestant denominations, no longer even believe in the deity of Jesus Christ. They most certainly do not accept His lordship, obeying what He commanded. They see no need for salvation since, in their view, there is no such thing as sin. "Evil" is caused by society's oppression, Big Business, greed, racism, etc. It is viewed, if anything, as a sickness, not as a result of a sinful heart which needs to be changed.

And because the reliability and veracity of the Bible is highly doubtful in their view, they must develop their own moral code, which changes and evolves consistent with the "political correctness" of the times. Relativism is everything; any type of absolute is condemned as narrow-minded, bigoted and intolerant, which are the supreme "sins" in these organizations.

These are undoubtedly the churches which will unite into one worldwide religious organization, aligning with the anti-Christ in the final years of this era, as predicted by John in the Book of Revelation. They may very well join with New Agers and other non-Christian religions as well, since there would be no major doctrinal barriers to such a union. This apostate church we see today is not the genuine Church, and God will eventually deal with them by eternally banishing them from His presence. They are rebels. They actually slander and blaspheme Jesus Christ by taking His name. It would be better for such false teachers to be drowned in the depths of the sea, Jesus said.

There are undoubtedly true Christians still attending these apostate churches. But those believers need to carefully assess whether their participation in such organizations is pleasing to God and whether they are receiving any spiritual nutrition therein. If not, they need to flee these organizations just as they would flee from a sinful activity. If you are truly His, Jesus said, you will recognize His voice and will not follow a "stranger," but will run from him because you do not recognize his voice. Churches change over the years, and just because mom, dad or grandparents were part of that particular organization does not mean that it is the true Church today, deserving of our time, energy and money.

These apostate churches are surely more offensive to God than even non-Christian religious organizations, because their false teachers take His name but do not follow His commandments or respect the written Word He has given to His Church. These churches are, of course, "mainstream" in Western society and for that reason are respected by the world. But remember what Jesus said of them, "You are those who justify yourselves before men but God knows your hearts. For what is highly esteemed among men is an abomination in the sight of God."

And He promises that in Heaven "there shall by no means enter it anything that defiles, or causes an abomination or a lie, but only those who are written in the Lamb's Book of Life."

EXTRA-BIBLICAL

The second group might be called "Bible-plus" churches. They accept the Bible as valid but, for one reason or many, have added other beliefs and teachings to their doctrines, which dilute or pervert it.

The Church of Jesus Christ of Latter-Day Saints (the Mormons) is a prime example of this second group. Possibly the fastest growing of any organization to call itself Christian, the Mormons added the Book of Mormon and many doctrines, which are not only absent from the pages of the Bible, but are even contrary to Scripture. For example, their founder, Joseph Smith, claimed that an angel gave him the Book of Mormon, which he added to the canon of Scripture. This was done despite the apostle Paul's strong admonition: "But even if...an angel from Heaven should preach a gospel other than the one we preach to you, let him be eternally condemned." Or Paul's discussion of "another Jesus" being preached, and warnings as to how "Satan himself masquerades as an angel of light." Or John's curse upon "anyone [who] adds anything to the words of...this Book."

There are many examples of gross doctrinal error the Mormons have developed by adding to the Bible. One of many examples is their teaching regarding elaborate marriage structures in the afterlife, which ignore the clear words of Jesus, who explained that there will be no marriage in the next life.

The Bible is merely one of several sources of doctrine for another, the Roman Catholic Church. Catholics teach, essentially, that church tradition and edicts from the leadership govern its membership and that a parishioner is saved by following the rites and requirements set forth by this church organizational system, developed over the centuries.

It is considered almost poor taste to even discuss incorrect Catholic doctrines these days. Differences are glossed over the for the sake of "Christian unity." But the fact is, many falsehoods are taught by this organization, doctrines that are harmful to the cause of Christ.

There is no historic support for their contention that the apostle Peter was ever a bishop of Rome, for example. Jesus strictly instructed that we should "not call anyone on earth 'father,' for you have only one Father, and He is in Heaven." This did not stop the Roman Catholic Church from developing the papistry, alleging that their line of popes trace back to Peter and declaring that these popes (many quite corrupt and several even aligned with evil political regimes) are infallible!

From the "infallible" word of these popes and their councils have developed doctrines quite contrary to the Bible. Purgatory, for example, never existed before the 13th century and did not become "dogma" until the 16th century. It is not mentioned anywhere in the Bible. Charles Spurgeon opined that Purgatory was invented as a means to gain finance for the corrupt Roman church. He called it "pick-pocket Purgatory" because it had robbed money from many poor souls (the decedent's family is strongly urged to pay the priest additional offerings, in order for him to pray that their loved one quickly passes from Purgatory into Heaven). Martin Luther poetically put it this way: "They preach human folly, who pretend that as soon as money in the copper rings, a soul from Purgatory springs." Importantly, the false doctrine of Purgatory misses the Biblical concept that Christ's work on the cross removed our punishment, that we do not suffer or work in order to gain entrance to Heaven, i.e., there are no sins to be "purged" for those who've put their faith in Christ Jesus.

The priesthood, as practiced by the Roman Catholic, Orthodox and some Protestant faiths, is also contrary to the Bible, which portrays only Christ as our Advocate with the Father. Indeed, Peter lays the "priesthood" mantle upon all Christian believers.

And, although Jesus called His mother "woman" and once even spurned her, preferring to be with His followers, Mary has been deified as a goddess, "the Queen of Heaven," by the Roman Catholic Church over the years, to the point of idolatry. What Dr. John MacArthur calls an "utterly pagan" view of Mary (whom Catholics often blasphemingly refer to as "the Mother of God") evolved over the centuries but intensified in the past century. Pope Leo XIII declared in 1891 that "no one can approach Christ except through his mother." Pope Pius XI alleged in 1923 that Mary "shared the work of redemption with Jesus Christ," and Pope Benedict XV in 1918 contended that she "redeemed the human race with Christ." Vatican II said, "Mary's intercession continues to win for us the gift of eternal salvation." Under Pope John Paul II, six million Catholics worldwide petitioned to have Mary declared "co-redemptrix" with Jesus Christ, as if it is a legislative matter. Although an avowed "Marian," the Pope backed down under media pressure and refrained from making such a proclamation. But again, even the very concept of fellow-sinner Mary serving as our advocate disregards the Bible teachings that there is only "one mediation — the Man Christ Jesus."

But it was the selling of "indulgences" (paying the Church in advance for such sins as adultery) and other extra-Biblical heresies that propelled the Protestant Reformation in the 1500s. The Church had become so corrupt, so removed from the teachings of the Bible, that many were willing to rebel and form churches outside the pope's domination, even at the risk of their own lives.

Does this mean that all Roman Catholics are going to Hell? Not at all! But they, and those outside, need to understand that many of their teachings have been invented and devised by men whose motives are highly questionable, to say the least.

Others would argue that several other groups who call themselves Christians also "add" to the written Word of God, the Holy Bible. By questionable prophecies, Charismatic believers sometimes tread on very thin ice by giving instructions to their congregations which may be adding or subtracting from the written Word of God. The Charismatic movement has mushroomed, crossing denominational lines into Protestant and Catholic churches. Some of these congregations rely more on emotional feeling and what they contend to be divine, personal revelation from God, rather than seeking out the sound doctrines set forth by the authors of the Bible. And, again, it has caused many tragic consequences, both on a personal and corporate level. It has even lead to cult-like following of charming men and women who convince and persuade by their gifted speech and presentation, but who are not truly of God. When the sound doctrine of Scripture is abandoned for pursuit of a personality, or trends of the moment, then "anything goes," and the result can be chaotic, destructive, and catastrophic, as many have learned the hard way.

Many of these so-called "prophecies" given in Charismatic churches are simply false. Speaking on behalf of God is a very serious matter. In the Old Testament, under the Jewish Law, false prophets were stoned to death. One wonders how many "prophecies" would be given in modern churches, if records were to be kept of their outcome, and the "false prophets" were to be put to death. Instead, "extra-Biblical," so-called "prophecies" are given freely in many of these types of churches without regard as to whether they are truly from God. If they are contrary to the Bible, you can most assuredly conclude that they are false. God would never contradict what is in His written Word.

Again, for true believers who are involved in such church organizations which add or subtract from the written Word of God, they should carefully examine whether to remain in such organizations or flee from them. They, too, should examine their own motives for staying within such organizations, if they clearly know them to be wrong.

BIBLE-CENTERED

The third "branch," if you will, of Christianity is one which maintains that the 66 books of the Bible are divinely inspired by God, written by men, filtered through their own personalities, but who knew Jesus personally or otherwise received direct revelation from God Himself. They believe the Bible is sufficient for all doctrine and revelation from God.

After all, Paul writes that Christ "wash[es us] with water through the Word." We are cleansed by reading and obeying what has been written for our instruction in the Bible. In doing so, we'll be able to present ourselves to Christ at the Judgment, "as a radiant church, without stain or wrinkle or any other blemish, but holy and blameless."

They remember that even Jesus made His arguments based on Old Testament Scripture, often quoting from it. In fact, He quoted the Bible to rebuke Satan at the time of His temptation in the desert, specifically quoting Deuteronomy 8:3, noting that "man does not live on bread alone but on every word that comes from the mouth of God." Peter, Paul and the other New Testament writers frequently interspersed Old Testament quotations in their preaching and writings, as well as quotations of Jesus. Paul wrote to his student and spiritual son Timothy, "All Scripture is God-breathed and is useful for teaching, rebuking, correcting and training in righteousness, so that the man of God may be thoroughly equipped for every good work." The first Church, we are told, devoted themselves "to the apostles' teaching," much of which we now recognize as the New Testament. They knew that only these men, the eleven plus Paul, were directly chosen by Christ to teach them His authentic, true doctrine and commandments. But even in those early days, Paul was constantly attacked by other false teachers who were satanic in nature, trying to lead the Church astray, persuading them to follow "another" gospel.

Jesus said that if we love Him, we will keep His commandments. And by what method do we know how to do that, but to study the Bible? He made a promise that, if we keep His commandments, God will love us, and that Jesus will love us and manifest Himself to us. So studying the Bible, and acting upon what you read, is the way to develop an intimate relationship with God. The Israelites were promised prosperity and success, if they would meditate on God's Book day and night, observing what was written in it. We can be spiritually wealthy by doing the same. That is how He chooses to reveal Himself to us.

It was in an attempt to return to this Bible-based theology that the Protestant reformers broke from a corrupt Roman church. Martin Luther, whose *95 Theses* sparked a religious fire the Roman Catholic Church was unable to extinguish, held to four principles. The theological conflict which ensued focused on the so-called four-fold "alones" of the reformation: *sola gratia, sola Christo, sola fide,* and *sola Scriptura* (salvation is by grace alone, in Christ alone, by faith alone, and all that is necessary for salvation is found in Scripture alone). These four "alones" served as a canon by which the teaching of the Roman Catholic Church was assessed and found to be wanting.

But sadly, even this return to the Bible did not bring a unity of the Christian faith in one sound, accepted doctrine. The Protestant movement, which was never totally unified to begin with, began splintering into thousands of pieces, each interpreting the Bible and doctrine in many different ways. Even though they all supposedly derive their doctrine from the same Book, they differ widely on such doctrines as: how one is saved (by faith vs. faith-plus-works); whether the life Christ gives is eternally secure (vs. salvation conditional upon behavior); what parts, if any, of the Old Testament Law must be kept; and whether the supernatural events and gifts prevalent in the early Church are for today.

In some cases, these doctrinal differences are fairly innocuous. Others, however, are so crucial to the orthodoxy of Christian faith that only some of these Bible believers can be correct and the others with opposing views must surely be fatally wrong. Some of these doctrines, although supposedly based upon the Bible, are errant to the point of heresy.

So we come full circle, realizing that even those who use only the Bible as their guide are not all true Christians, and that the Lord will surely have to sort them all out — those who are truly His own, separated from those who are mistaken or merely pretending to be His followers.

To the outsiders, these doctrinal differences must be terribly confusing, because they are admittedly confusing even to those who claim the name of Christ. On top of that, people of other religions look at the sinful decadence of a so-called Christian nation like the United States of America and decide they want no part of that!

But Christ Himself did not leave us without warning. Throughout His ministry on earth, He warned over and over again that there would be false teachers who would lead many astray. So it is incumbent upon any individual who wishes to be a true follower of Christ to pray, seeking wisdom from above. James writes, "If any of you lack wisdom, let him ask of God who gives to all liberally and without reproach, and it will be given to him." I do not think that God wants us to be ignorant about what church organization or doctrines we should be affiliated with. After all, our eternal destiny may depend upon our view of Christ, and what He requires. Therefore, if we ask and allow Him to, He will give us His Holy Spirit to guide us with regard to what doctrines are correct. He will lead us to those with whom we should fellowship and worship.

But, if we are content in simply following tradition, continuing in the way we were brought up to believe, or attempting to please the world and follow the crowd, then He will not interfere; He will allow us to continue on our path toward destruction.

To that puzzled outsider goes this explanation: *not all those that claim to be Christian churches really are.* Please judge Jesus Christ by what you read of Him in Scripture, rather than what you often see coming from these so-called churches who are following false teachers. They do not represent Christ, and He will deal with them in His own way, in His own time.

Myth 7:
Everything Claiming to Be Christian Really Is

Americans have realized during the past several decades that people in Third World nations often have a distorted perspective of us because of what they see in movies produced in this country. When foreign audiences see Americans portrayed only as decadent, wealthy, or violent people who enjoy destruction and war, etc., they get a false impression of what real life is for the overwhelming majority of us who live in this nation. Surely we all could agree that Hollywood does not depict our normal, everyday lives!

Similarly, during the past 2000 years, critics have often held a distorted view of Christianity based on events and the behavior of some people. They see individuals, even nations, who have taken the mantle of Christianity upon themselves but who have not acted very Christ-like.

They cite such "non-Christian behavior" for their refusal to have anything to do with the Church. It is sometimes a reason they ban Christian missionaries. If they have not read the Bible or studied what Christ really taught, they know only what they have observed or heard secondhand about Christianity. And much of that has not been a very pleasant sight; in fact, much has been a disgrace to the name of Jesus.

There are many examples of non-Christian behavior throughout the twenty centuries of Church history, but four of those are most often cited.

CHURCH WEALTH

One of the first criticisms of the Church is that it possesses great wealth, which its critics contend could and should be shared with the world's poor.

They point to the billions of dollars' worth of art and treasure in the Vatican, real estate holdings worldwide, and other investments and holdings of the Roman Catholic Church. Likewise, many Orthodox and Protestant organizations have gathered immense wealth over the years. The building of larger, more elaborate edifices to draw larger congregations is the world's measure of success, which often has been adopted by church leaders. Sadly, Christianity is being handled more and more like any other business, rather than a ministry of mercy and light, as was intended and mandated by Jesus. Particularly irritating to believers and nonbelievers alike are some of the television and radio ministries, which have made their leaders very, very rich, sometimes via highly questionable methods, and in which many espouse false doctrines.

Even nonbelievers instinctively know that accumulation of such massive fortunes by religious organizations, by preying upon the poor, the elderly, and the gullible, is contrary to the teachings of Christ. The situation is indefensible; it is a blot upon Christianity, a disgrace. Moreover, it detracts from the fact that the Church has been the most charitable organization in history.

NOT WHAT JESUS TAUGHT

Wealthy holdings by churches do not square with the commands of Jesus. There is no indication in the New Testament that God wants His Church to accumulate wealth, either on a personal or corporate basis, and there's much to indicate that He is quite opposed to the concept.

Some of the most truly successful ministries in the history of the Church — those which spiritually feed their flocks, change lives and win new converts — have been of humble origin and status. Some do not even possess any real estate at all. Their congregations meet in homes, storefronts, warehouses, etc., even quietly and secretly in some parts of the world. Their leaders often work for low wages or even volunteer their services.

Jesus was clearly "anti-wealth." Revisionists, defensive of the riches of many of today's churches, mention that Jesus' disciples carried a moneybag, as if that proves that they were well off financially. But they ignore the fact that Jesus, by His own admission, had no place to even lay His head during His ministry. He probably built houses for others as a carpenter, but He had none for Himself. And, unlike exempt religious organizations in the United States, Jesus even paid taxes!

Jesus told the rich young ruler that, in order to become perfect, he should sell all of his possessions, give the proceeds to the poor, and follow Him. It is easier for a camel to go through the eye of a needle than for a rich man to enter the Kingdom of Heaven, Jesus proclaimed. Jesus spoke of the "deceitfulness of riches," and Paul warned that the Church should not "trust in uncertain riches." The pursuit of riches can choke us, Jesus explained, distracting us from what is really important in life.

The apostles certainly were not rich. "Gold and silver have I none," confessed Peter. Jesus had instructed His disciples to "live off the land," accepting contributions from those to whom they preached. Paul disclosed that he was impoverished during most of his missionary work, had even gone without clothing and food at times. He worked as a tent-maker in some of the towns in which he preached, to support himself.

The apostles frowned upon anyone who tried to get rich through Christianity. Simon, formerly a magician, wanted to buy the gift of healing. Of course that was impossible and Peter scolded him, "May your money perish with you...! You have no part or share in this ministry because your heart is not right before God." In another example, Ananias and his wife Sapphira were struck dead by God for lying about the portion of money that they were contributing to the Church! God dealt harshly in that first Church with those who wished to mix their greed with this new religious faith, probably in order to send a strong message on the subject.

Rather than seeking riches here on earth, Jesus urged His followers to do those things which would earn treasures for them in Heaven, which will last forever, as a reward from God for doing good works. Jesus promised if we use our time and financial resources to feed the hungry, clothe the needy and help those who are sick or in prison, He will credit it to our account as having done that for Him, and that we will be rewarded for those actions in the next life. He reminded us, too, that our wealth here on earth is subject to decay and theft.

Jesus cautioned that those who seek earthly wealth fail to be mindful of the things above: "For where your treasure is, there will your heart be also." He added that we cannot serve God and money at the same time; one or the other is always going to be our master. Either the love of money *or* the love of God is ruling your life and mine, right now. Even if one could somehow gain all of the wealth in the world, it would not be an equal trade for His soul, Jesus emphasized.

Materially, the Church in the last days of this era will be a very rich one, John prophesied but, spiritually, it will be poor. (We're likely in that era now or soon will enter it.) John quotes Jesus as saying about this "Church of Laodicea," which many think is symbolic of the Church's final era:

> *You say, 'I am rich: I have acquired wealth and do not need a thing.' But you do not realize that you are wretched, pitiful, poor, blind and naked. I counsel*

> *you to buy from me gold refined in the fire, so you can become rich; and white clothes to wear, so you can cover your shameful nakedness; and salve to put on your eyes, so you can see.*

James wrote of these wealthy people and condemned them. James further admonished the Church not to show favoritism to the wealthy. And he warned the rich man that "he will pass away like a wildflower." He added, "For the sun rises with scorching heat and withers the plants; its blossom falls and its beauty is destroyed. And the same way, the rich man will fade away even while he goes about his business."

James attacked the wealthy mercilessly:

> *Now listen, you rich people, weep and wail because of the misery that is coming upon you. Your wealth has rotted, and moths have eaten your clothes. Your gold and silver are corroded. Their corrosion will testify against you and eat your flesh like fire. You have hoarded wealth in the last days. Look! The wages you failed to pay the workmen who mowed your fields are crying out against you. The cries of the harvesters have reached the ears of the Lord Almighty. You have lived on earth in luxury and self-indulgence. You have fattened yourselves in the day of slaughter.*

Jesus once physically exhibited how He felt about those who would use religion to become rich. Without meekness or mildness — uncharacteristically — He went through the Temple area (with a whip!) and drove out all of those who were buying and selling there. He overturned the tables of the moneychangers and the benches of those selling sacrificial doves. "It is written," He yelled at them, "My house will be called a house of prayer, but you are making it a 'den of robbers.'"

The unbelieving world has the right to be distrusting, even disdainful of what it perceives to be representative of the Church when it sees the greed exhibited by many throughout the centuries.

But does it sound to you, in reviewing these Bible passages, that Jesus would approve of the massive, elaborate cathedrals and church buildings, expensive church art, glamorous television production settings, huge mansions, private jets, extravagant limousines, designer clothing and well-padded stock portfolios of various so-called church leaders? People and organizations that are in the "greed business" absolutely are not in conformity with true Christianity. God is undoubtedly disgusted with it, and He will judge these people in due time.

In the meantime, we should not judge the *true* Church by the actions of these greedy individuals. They are not representative of Jesus Christ.

COLONIALISM

Standard fare among Western historians in this era of political correctness is to teach students more and more about (non-Christian) Asian and African cultures and history and de-emphasize traditional themes which explain European and American development. A reader is more likely to find a chapter on North African desert trade routes in the 13th Century than about the Elizabethan Era, for example. And when you do get to read about European and American history, the emphasis has shifted. Western culture is more likely depicted as preying upon, exploiting and even destroying indigenous peoples, rather than having brought medicine, education, civilization, order and better methods to these cultures, as we once viewed ourselves as having accomplished. As the result of this modern view, Christian Europeans become the villains and vandals and the indigenous people are the victims.

There is, of course, some truth to this revisionism. The Spaniards, for example, killed many of the native people in

Central and South America, both by the sword and disease, stole their land, their gold and other wealth, and imposed their language, culture, dress and religion upon these people who had not even invited them to their country. The English and French did nearly the same to the natives of North America. It is difficult, if not impossible, to fully defend all of what our forefathers have done.

But many of these revisionists have gone a step further, demanding an end to Christian missionary work altogether, contending that it destroys ancient cultures. They want proselytizing to be criminalized. They will likely soon succeed; the United Nations has petitions before it from time to time to criminalize missionary efforts, as already has happened in several nations. Christians in some countries, particularly Islamic countries, are permitted to provide free or low-cost health services, for example, but are not allowed to discuss Jesus with non-Christians or invite them to church.

These enemies of missionary work are upset that, when jungle or island people become followers of Christ, they often become "Westernized," adapting to our style of clothing, personal hygiene, monogamy, and so forth. Never mind that some of these people were going naked and following such unusual "marital" customs that their children had no idea who their parents were. Forget that many of these people once sacrificed children, women and captured enemies to their gods. Ignore the fact that some of these tribes spent much of their time at war and even collected heads of their enemies, before being converted to Christianity. These "customs" should be respected, the "political correctness police" contend; we shouldn't seek to reform them. Sometimes Christian missionaries are just teaching basic decency and human kindness — lessons such as, "Don't kill your handicapped babies" — or showing tribes how to obtain clean water or to avoid disease-transmitting sources.

And it doesn't matter to these critics that most of what we consider civilized behavior in Western society — peaceful government, courts, religious freedom, fairness, caring for the poor, human rights, even democracy itself — has its roots in Judeo-Christian culture. They discount the fact that such a system is beneficial even for those who are not Christians or Jews.

But to the extent that the Christians have proselytized at the point of a sword ("convert or die"), as the Spanish reportedly did in Columbus' day, it was totally, absolutely wrong, and contrary to the teachings of Jesus Christ. The fact that other religions such as the Muslims have violently forced conversions to their faith, by the millions, and continue to do so to this very day, does not justify the rare cases of forceful conversions in Christendom's history.

Jesus did command His followers, "Go into all the world and preach the good news to all creation." He directed that we preach repentance and forgiveness in His name "to all nations, beginning at Jerusalem." Missionary work in Christianity is something believers are *required* by their Lord to do and to support. They have no choice but to do so if they are obedient; they cannot keep the Gospel quiet. Talking to friends, family, colleagues about Jesus is something *all* believers should do, in addition to financially and prayerfully helping spread the Gospel throughout the world. He wants us to politely and gently "confess" Him before men and women at every opportunity. We do not know who will accept the Gospel or reject it. But He most certainly did not command His followers to even come close to coercion as they attempt to persuade others of the rightness of their cause, or the need for salvation.

Instead, Jesus considered the Gospel to be a precious gift, "a pearl of great price," to be shared with others. But if these people to whom the Gospel is preached in a particular area refuse it and do not welcome the messengers, then Jesus told them to shake the very dust off their feet when they depart those towns, and preach it somewhere else, sowing seeds in fertile, receptive soil instead. Indeed, He even cautioned against wasting time on people who are unreceptive to the Gospel, who treat it with disdain. Don't throw your pearls to the pigs, Jesus admonished His disciples: don't waste your time on them, if they do not want to hear the Gospel or accept the invitation. All of this is a far cry from forcing, even strongly persuading, nonbelievers to become Christians.

Nor are Christians in any way guided by the Bible to colonialize other people or to change their cultures (except to the extent that we should persuade them to live holy lives). To the contrary, Paul (by then, Christian in culture) said that he had done nothing "against the customs" practiced by his Jewish ancestors in Israel. Paul said he became "a slave to everyone to win as many as possible. To the Jews I became like a Jew, to win the Jews." It can safely be assumed that he did not go against the cultural lifestyles of other countries in which he preached; he was respectful of them. For this first, and most important, Christian missionary, culture was not what mattered. Paul wanted to change hearts, not the community or ethnic styles of living.

With regard to seizure of other peoples' land and personal property, that, too, is an extreme contradiction to what Jesus taught. He preached that His followers should be givers, not takers; generous and gracious, not greedy and thieving. He went to the extreme of demanding that Christians even love their enemies, do good to those who hate them, bless those who curse them, turn the other cheek to those who strike them — even suggesting that if someone demands your jacket, you should give him your overcoat, too.

Colonialization, destroying national cultures and histories, stealing from them, are all concepts foreign to the New Testament. They are as old as humankind and originate in greed, racism, pride, hatred, and covetousness and are common to all cultures and nationalities — certainly not limited to Christians or Europeans. Africans, Asians and Native Americans did it to each other, long before the Europeans came along.

These concepts most certainly are not part of true Christianity and never have been. Preaching the Gospel to all the world, however, did originate with Jesus. Unfortunately, Christian missionary work has too often become intertwined with political and cultural goals, much to the detriment of the Gospel message among the people to whom it was delivered.

But those who have confused "Westernization" with spreading the Gospel have simply been mistaken. Many in the Third World nations believe that Christianity and the West are synonymous. They don't even realize that Christianity started as a Middle Eastern, Asian religion. They incorrectly view it as European and American, a "white man's religion."

The Bible tells us that God is no respecter of persons. During this Gentile Era, He shows no favoritism toward particular nationalities or cultures. His Church should do the same. But it should never be forced to hide its full message or the need for personal holiness in daily living, for example, in the name of political correctness, just because it might offend someone. When people invite Christ into their lives, it sometimes does change their culture, simply because believers' lifestyles must measure up to His holy standards. And as long as people are allowed to make free choices in that regard, such missionary work should not be stifled.

THE CRUSADES

I once had a crusty old national radio commentator surprise me by replying, on the air, to my e-mailed invitation that he consider Christ. He responded by jeering, "But what about all those wars that have been fought in the name of Christianity?" In his case, he was probably just making an excuse for a lifestyle which he does not want to change. But in doing so, he threw out a reason many have cited for doubting the sincerity of Christians, based on the Church's past. He may have been remembering a line from a 1970s song, "So many people have died in the name of Christ that I can't believe it all."

As we know, there have been "holy wars" throughout the millennia, by and between Muslims, Jews and hundreds of other religious groups. But somehow people expect pacifism and submissiveness from the people who call themselves Christian.

Perhaps it's because of Jesus' call to "turn the other cheek," or for His followers to be meek and forgiving, which causes them to expect something different from Christians. They are disillusioned and disappointed when they consider the part of Church history called "the Crusades".

For those who were asleep that day in history class, I remind you that the religion known as Islam arose in the Arabian Peninsula in the 7th Century. It instructed its followers to bring the world under the political control and domination of leaders who were faithful to Islam. Even in Mohammed's day, they were fighting wars of conquest. Islam's military and political rule was spread by the sword, as continues to occur today in parts of the world.

The Koran, the Islamic holy book, recommends that Muslims not take Christians and Jews as friends, but that they fight against Christians and Jews until they submit to Allah or else agree to a specific tax. It also refers to Jews as "apes and swine to be despised and rejected." Islam, for that and other reasons, has a special hatred for Western society and has fought it for centuries on the battlefields.

Within a century of Mohammad's death, Islam had split into warring sects, such as the Shiites and the Sunnis. In the 700s A.D. they began conquering the entire Middle East, parts of Central Asia and India, as well as North Africa. By 710 A.D. they had even taken the majority of territory in Spain and Portugal, as well as Sicily and one-third of France. For decades there were protracted military struggles between the nations dominated by the Christian faith and those ruled by Muslims, and the outcome of those wars was far from certain. Driven out of Europe, they made a second effort to subjugate all of that continent in the 17th century, when the Turks began to expand their Ottoman Empire, taking Greece, the former Yugoslavia, Bulgaria and parts of Romania and Hungary, before they were driven back. Much of the struggle was about land and wealth, obviously, but it was rooted deeply in religious conflict as well.

Against this backdrop, and urged on by several of the popes

(who were strong political and military leaders in Europe at the time), several thousands of Europeans invaded Jerusalem under Christian banners, beginning in the summer of 1096 A.D. There were several crusades and counter-crusades. Possession of Palestine shifted back and forth between Christians and Muslims, causing the loss of tens of thousands of lives and untold resources. Although the Crusades wound down in the 1600s, the war actually continues, to date, in places like the former Yugoslavia, the Far East, and elsewhere. And, to this day, you will find very little religious freedom or tolerance in Muslim countries.

No doubt the Crusaders were trying to "do God's work" or perhaps even thought they could hasten the Second Coming of Christ by retaking the spot (Jerusalem) where He had promised to return to earth. But they were following the direction of kings, popes and other earthly leaders, not the Word of God, in doing so.

After all, Jesus made it clear at several points that His is a *spiritual*, not a political, kingdom, at least in this era. He specifically instructed His disciples not to fight for Him. When Peter tried to prevent Jesus' arrest and sliced off a guard's ear, Jesus healed the victim and scolded Peter, "Put your sword back in its place, for all who draw the sword will die with a sword." (It was God's will that Jesus go to the cross and He did not want to forcefully prevent that.) But note, Jesus did not tell Peter to get rid of His sword, but merely to put it back into its sheath.

Self-defense is morally different than aggression, obviously. While Jesus instructed us to love our enemies, nothing He said, or that the New Testament authors wrote, prevents a Christian from engaging in self-defense. The Bible, from cover-to-cover, advocates keeping order by police and military action. Such authorities are established by God; policeman and soldiers are even servants of God, Paul wrote. It might shock some to recall that Jesus told His disciples to take their swords with them, and if they did not have swords to even sell their coats to buy one. (Look it up — Luke 22:36.) He urged them to arm themselves for protection; today's equivalent would be to carry a handgun!

No, Jesus did not endorse total pacifism; He just preached against a retaliatory or aggressive attitude.

Perhaps the European invasion of Palestine was wrong — there's no question that, with God's sovereign protection, the Church could have survived even if Europe had fallen to the Muslims. In fact, the Church has seemed to flourish and even become stronger under persecution as occurred in its early days under the Roman Empire and as is witnessed by the millions of Christian converts in China today.

The Church had been intertwined in politics since Constantine made it the official religion of the Roman Empire, which was not necessarily a positive development. It became involved in political rule much to its detriment and quite contrary to God's will.

But Christendom need make no excuse for defending its homelands in centuries past. Nor should Christian nations apologize for ridding the world of Nazism and Japanese imperialism, resisting the imperialistic expansion of atheistic Communism, taking out bullies and despots like Saddam Hussein, or even trying militarily to destroy terrorism in modern times.

Grievous mistakes have been made by leaders calling themselves Christians over the past 2000 years, however. No question, some very evil people have wrapped their greed, covetousness and prideful conquests in religious cloaks to the disrepute of Jesus Christ and His true Church.

But to reject Jesus on the basis of what happened hundreds of years ago in the Crusades, or in other "Christian wars," is such a weak excuse as to be laughable. It is the height of absurdity to hold Christians to such an unreasonable, illogical standard of non-Biblical pacifism.

Refusing to consider Jesus Christ because of what happened centuries ago in the Crusades is akin to renouncing your United States citizenship because of atrocities our country committed during the Vietnam or the American Civil War. Sorry, but you'll need to come up with a better excuse than that!

The Inquisition

Yet another subject cited as a reason to distrust Christianity is what was known as the "Inquisition". Again, for the benefit of those who missed discussion of the Inquisition in their history classes, a brief review is offered.

The Inquisition began in 1478 in Spain when, at the request of King Ferdinand and Queen Isabella, Pope Sixtus IV issued a papal bull for the creation of the Spanish Inquisition. It was not abolished until 1834, although its most fervent activity occurred during the 1400s and the 1500s.

It caused a reign of bloody terror which spread into Portugal and throughout Europe. Countless Jews, Muslims and "heretical" Christians (those who did not follow all of the pope's and Roman Catholic Church's orders) were tortured unmercifully and killed in cruel ways, their property stolen from them. In many cases, the Inquisition, operated by both civil and church authority, rooted out those who did not conform to Roman Catholic law.

Actually, the Spanish Inquisition was just a continuation of earlier papal inquisitions initiated by Pope Gregory IX in 1231. And in 1542, Pope Paul III established the Congregation of the Inquisition to pursue Protestants. Again, many of the Protestant "heretics" were tortured and killed. Sadly, rather than learning a lesson from this experience, some Protestants later became as bad as the Catholics in persecuting Jews, Catholics and other Protestants with whom they disagreed. It was due to both Roman Catholic and Protestant persecution that many early settlers fled to America.

Throughout these centuries of the Inquisitions, much emphasis was placed upon finding and executing "witches" and "sorcerers," which of course was heavily dependent upon subjective identification. As was seen when this "witch hunt" extended into New England in the 1600s, targets of these religious zealots were often just non-conformists and undoubtedly many were victims of sadists and sexual perverts who pretended that they were acting on God's behalf.

And, again, this dark, scary, evil era of Christendom has no connection whatever to the teachings of Jesus, the Bible, or His true Church.

Jesus often cautioned His followers about following false teachers; that much is true. And He stressed the necessity of obeying God's commands. He also sanctioned the establishment of a Church and, presumably, its government. But He never even remotely suggested torturing or killing these so-called "heretics."

Likewise, Paul used much ink to harshly condemn false teachers who were perverting the Gospel, often based upon greedy, personal power motives. Paul urged the churches which he had established to maintain a strict disciplinary process in their membership. He did not want these churches to tolerate heretics in their midst, knowing that it would contaminate the Church and lead it astray, as has happened. But Paul's solution to a disobedient church member was to oust him from the church, to excommunicate him, until he repented. Paul emphasized that even this was to be done gently, prayerfully, with humility and grace. He never even came close to prescribing torture, execution or other persecution of such people. Nor did he advocate forcefully converting or reforming them, such as occurred in the Roman Catholic or early Protestant churches.

The practices occurring during the Inquisition most certainly were not Bible-based. As is true today, when one departs from written Scripture, there is a danger of getting involved in all types of evil, as occurred during that infamous era.

Like the Crusades, the Inquisition is a terrible blot upon the history of the Church. But it was not, by any stretch of the imagination, Christian in its essence. To the contrary, it was one of Satan's greatest accomplishments. Nothing pleases Satan more than to invade the Bride of Christ — the Church — and infiltrate it with his own, in an attempt to bring shame upon Jesus Christ, who will someday destroy him. He loves to see infighting and self-destruction in the Church.

And Satan will succeed at least one more time in the future.

The Bible predicts that there will be a false, worldwide "church" during the Great Tribulation, lead by a false, satanic leader with supernatural powers. And again, Jews and true Christians will then be persecuted and killed by this false "church." The concept of such an evil "church," either in the Middle Ages, or in the future, is the antithesis of the true Church, however.

***

There are many other examples which could be cited. So-called Christian right-wing militias who take up arms against law enforcement and other government officers, preaching violence, are one such example. Or left-wingers who use the pulpits of so-called Christian churches to advocate environmental extremism, vegetarianism, socialism and who rail against the corporations. Or the racists of all colors who "use" the Church as their platform for hatred, as well as "Christian" cults that draw families into dangerous, sometimes insane behavior.

Certainly, an entire book could be written about the sin of anti-Semitism by so-called Christians over the centuries. The evil done against His chosen race will not go unpunished by Almighty God.

Jesus would most likely say to these misguided, errant people who have misused His name, "My kingdom is not of this world." He would talk about grace, mercy, gentleness, and forgiveness.

Nonbelievers simply need to understand that not everything or everyone claiming the name of Christ is Christian. Jesus warned us that this would occur, but He will sort it all out at the Judgment. Those who did evil in His name will receive the worst punishment, I strongly believe.

In the meantime, we need to return to the pages of the Bible and study what Jesus actually taught, what He commanded, what He requires. Let us separate that correct picture from the one painted by His enemies within the Church.

MYTH 8:
CHRISTIANITY IS JUST LIKE OTHER RELIGIONS

They have modernized a bit since then, but the churches which I attended as a young man (upon command of my parents) were stuck in a culture somewhere between the 17th and the 19th Centuries. Similar to the Amish, men generally wore dark suits and white shirts to church services, the more devout ones wearing no ties and their shirts buttoned to the neck. Hair was kept short, and they had no facial hair.

The dress code for women was stricter. They were strongly urged not cut their hair. Dresses (never pants!) must be long. No jewelry or ornamentation. Sleeves were expected to be full length for both men and women. (I was once scolded by the youth leader for coming to church on a steamy August day in short sleeves.) There was to be absolutely no work on Sundays. No TV's, dancing, movies, ever. Even ball games were frowned upon. Smoking and drinking were very high on their list of "worst sins." There was a lot of talk about the evils of "worldliness" and the virtues of being "old-fashioned" (although I never found the latter referred to in my Bible) among these churches which descended from John Wesley.

No one in those churches actually stated that one had to dress or act that way to earn salvation, of course, but that was inferred and there was intense pressure to conform. Most attendees either did conform or depart; dissent was not encouraged. The congregations were understandably small, generally 50 to 100, many of whom were extended families. Although these well-intentioned folk would never have admitted it, there was a lot of cult-like controlling behavior going on (which caused much long-term psychological and spiritual harm to many). There was a lot of pride in being what they thought was God's elite, holy people, the only truly obedient ones. There was tremendous emphasis in each sermon upon "holy living," lest you slip and go to Hell. God would only tolerate so much misbehavior before He would give up on us, these "hell-fire preachers" would sternly warn.

I have read in amazement about Roman Catholics in Latin America who would crawl on their bleeding knees on cobblestone roads to some shrine in order to please God. Or a Phillipino who actually had himself nailed to a cross once a year to pay for his sins. Or about Catholics who would physically torture and even mutilate themselves in lesser ways in attempts to rid themselves of sin or evil tendencies, or to please God and their church. I would read of Orthodox Jews with their strict Sabbath-keeping, dietary rules and their version of the odd dress code. And the Muslims with their dress codes which in some areas required heavy veils and robes, covering women's bodies and faces completely, and their frequent prayers to the East and required pilgrimages to Mecca. Or the Eastern religions with their ornate temples, candles and incense, chanting, dances, memorizations, meditation, fasts, temple sacrifices, long pilgrimages to gurus, holy rivers and sites, and so forth. Then there were the ancient cultures in Africa, the Pacific and the Americas, with their complex attempts to please their gods, including human sacrifices.

None of the leaders of my boyhood churches would have ever made any remote connection between their own strict codes of conduct and those of other religions. Instead, they would find some Bible verse (often taken out of context) to support their strict rules of conduct. It would not have occurred to them that all were doing essentially the same thing in their own way: *trying to work their way to Heaven.*

WHEN HAVE I DONE ENOUGH?

So much uncertainty, even anxiety, results from these "works" religions. Unanswered questions gnaw at you. How much "good" do I have to perform to be acceptable to God? How much of that good is negated by my sinful or lazy behavior? If my good must outweigh my bad in order to please God, how is that measured? Is it like, two good deeds cancel out one sin? And what if I live a holy life for many years but then "blow it" all by sinning just before I die? When my salvation depends on me, how can I be sure that I am ever saved, since I can never predict what I might do?

But what makes true, Biblical Christianity different from all other religions of the world is that a believer does not "work" his way to Heaven, either by performing good deeds or abstaining from bad ones.

I'd always heard about God's grace, but never really understood it until I began to study the subject as an adult. Grasping what grace really meant was mind-boggling, almost impossible to accept, especially after being saturated in such a legalistic background for two decades.

"For it is by grace that you have been saved, through faith — and this not from yourselves, it is the gift of God — not by works, so that no one can boast," wrote Paul. I remember when the full meaning of that verse sunk in for the first time. It sounded too good to be true! You mean, I don't have to *do* anything to earn salvation? Just put my faith in Christ? It did not seem possible. It took many months for me to accept this truth.

Growing up in these "works" type churches, I had heard that "the Gospel" meant "the Good News." You'd hear a lot about the proclamation of the Good News, especially at Christmas. But, while in this legalistic, "works" environment, I thought, "What's so good about it?" I knew that I was a sinful person, susceptible to temptation. When I was honest with myself, I knew that I could never live a perfectly holy life. Perhaps I could live up to someone else's standards, but certainly I could never be good enough to remain in good standing with a righteous, holy God.

And, indeed, Paul wrote that people who try to work to keep the Law of God are under a curse, because we cannot do all that's required of us, no matter how hard we try. Instead, to the Roman Church he explained that "to the man who does not work but trusts God to justify the wicked, his faith is credited as righteousness," just as it had been for King David and Abraham. How could that be? Because Jesus "was delivered over to death for our sins and was raised to life for our justification." And, "since we have been justified through faith, we have peace with God through our Lord Jesus Christ, through whom we have gained access by faith into this grace in which we now stand." We are not "justified by the works of the law, but by faith in Jesus Christ," Paul explained.

The wages of sin is death, Paul continued. We were under a death sentence but Jesus did 100% of the required "work" by dying in our stead. I finally began to understand that the death of Jesus on the cross satisfied *all* of the punishment for *all* the sins of everyone who trusted in Him. He has reconciled those of us who were once enemies of God, alienated from Him, because of our wicked deeds.

We are chosen by grace, Paul continually reemphasizes, "And if by grace, then it is no longer by works; if it were, grace would no longer be grace." So we cannot mix grace and works, you see? We are saved by one or the other. And Paul correctly contends that no one is able to achieve, or maintain, acceptable standing with God through his works. None of us can be good enough or remain good enough to satisfy His holy demands.

Someone once made an apt analogy regarding what we might view as holy living vs. God's perfectly holy standard, His requirements. It would be like us mistakenly thinking that shooting an arrow 50 yards into the air would be a sufficiently impressive feat, when actually the target is the moon! We cannot even come close to being perfectly holy through our own works. We might think we are; we might even be proud of how righteous we have become, especially in comparing ourselves to others. But our righteous acts are like "filthy rags" in God's sight, Isaiah wrote.

This life in Christ is not meant to be a torturous one. We do not have to suffer self-punishment to pay for own sins. Christ already did that for us. We can rest in His grace, doing good works because we *want* to, not because we must do so. In almost every way, living for Christ is an easier, more pleasant road than the alternative. "My yoke is easy and my burden is light," Jesus promised.

SO WHY NOT KEEP SINNING?

Once you understand that we receive eternal life through faith in Christ alone, and that nothing else — good deeds, refraining from bad deeds, church membership, church rituals, penance, self-denial, anything we do — saves us, then the obvious question is always raised: then what difference does it make whether we continue in a sinful lifestyle? If God's grace covers all the sin of those who believe in His Son, then what does it matter? Some even fear that this "grace doctrine" will lead to moral irresponsibility.

First, if we still desire to lead a sinful lifestyle after we have become a Christian, we should question whether we truly have surrendered our life to Christ, whether our faith is genuine. John says, "We know that we have come to know Him if we obey His commands." He adds that, if we still love the things of this world, "the love of the Father is not in [us]," and that those who continue in a sinful lifestyle are "of the devil."

And Paul anticipated this very question in his letter to the Roman church. "What shall we say, then? Shall we go on sinning so that grace may increase? By no means! We died to sin; how can we live in it any longer?" Paul goes on to explain that the true Christian has joined Christ in death, and just as Christ was raised from the dead, "we too may live a new life." We should no longer be "slaves to sin," because we "have been set free from sin and have become slaves to righteousness." To the Corinthian Church, Paul explained, "Therefore, if anyone is in Christ, he is a new creation; the old has gone, the new has come!" A continued sinful lifestyle, Paul points out, leads to death, but the Christian should be living a lifestyle which leads to life, doing the good things which will count for all eternity.

James writes that we do not even possess true faith unless we have good works to accompany it. Faith without works is dead, he writes several times. One should question whether he has even come to a saving knowledge of Christ if he is not producing fruits of the Spirit and doing some type of activity for the Kingdom of God.

Peter prophesied that some day "the elements will be destroyed by fire and the earth and everything in it will be laid bare." All these things which we incorrectly think are so important now and strive for — fame, fortune, power, pleasure — will eventually come to nothing, either by our own death or by the end of this era. Even if you've reached great prominence in this world — perhaps they have even named a university building or a street in your honor — what does it all really mean in the long-term? Almost no one will even remember who you were 50 years after your death. Even so, what good will that respect and fame do you after you are dead? Eventually all of it will be destroyed anyway, says Peter.

REWARDS TO THE FAITHFUL

On the other hand, there is eternal value for a Christian in doing good works, which includes living a holy life, helping spread the Gospel, helping those in need, teaching and nurturing other Christians, sacrificing his time and resources. We should all "do good...be rich in good deeds...generous and willing to share."

For you see, each true Christian will some day appear before the Judgment Seat of Christ, at which time "each one may receive what is due him for the things done while in the body, whether good or bad." That Judgment will "bring to light" whether we have spent our lives building with "gold, silver, costly stone, wood, hay or straw; [our] work will be shown for what it is...." Like a goldsmith, Christ will then test each individual Christian's works by fire and, "if what he has built survives, he will receive his reward. If it is burned up, he will suffer loss; he himself will be saved, but only as one escaping through the flames." We will be held accountable for what we have done in this life, what we have done for Christ and our fellow man, even those of us who have accepted His gift of eternal life and secured our destiny.

Throughout His ministry, Jesus stressed that we do not want to come before Him having done nothing eternally profitable with our lives. Not only will it be a supreme embarrassment, a terrible disgrace, to stand before Him with nothing to show for our years on earth, but also there will be eternal consequences. Throughout His comments on the subject, Jesus made it clear that we will be given greater responsibility and riches in the next life, in accordance with what we did with the time, resources and opportunities He allotted to us in this life. By doing good works, Christians will "lay up treasure for themselves as a firm foundation for the coming age, so that they may take hold of the life that is truly life."

Christianity is not the only religion which believes in one God. Others, including Jews and Muslims, are monotheistic; even the followers of false gods such as Baal were that. And Christians are not the only ones who believe in performing good works. What makes true Christianity different from all other world religions is that we do not "work our way to Heaven," knowing that such a quest is impossible. Instead, Christians believe that the Son of God came to this earth, died a sacrificial death to pay for all of the sins of those who will believe in Him, and that those believers are thus made righteous in the eyes of our Creator and Judge, through faith alone.

And yes, true Christians believe that theirs is an exclusive way, that following Jesus Christ is the only way to God and eternal life. Call it bigotry, narrow-mindedness, intolerance, or what you will, but we cannot deny what our Lord plainly said: that He alone is *the* Way, *the* Truth, and *the* Life, and that no one comes to the Father except through Him. And think about it: if God gave His Son, a part of Himself, to die a cruel, humiliating death as payment for all sins for those who believe in Him, offering this free gift and this easy yoke, why would He allow entry into His Kingdom through any other door?

So what happens to all of those who reject Christ? Will they all burn in the Lake of Fire forever?

Just as there are degrees of reward to Christian believers, it is my opinion that there will be degrees of punishment to those who have not accepted Christ. God is the ultimate just and fair Judge. I trust that He will do what is correct and fair in each case, as each individual appears before Him in that day of final judgment. But I also believe that the worse punishment is reserved for those who know the truth, who have heard the offer of Jesus Christ time and time again, but have refused it. There will be no excuse in that day; we will not be able to blame others for our failure to investigate and accept Jesus Christ. There will be virtually no excuse for those who live in Western nations; they have heard the Gospel again and again. Life is very short and each of us must make a choice. By not accepting Jesus Christ, one has already made a choice.

It really comes down to only two alternatives, the Bible teaches. Either we are serving Jesus Christ and have surrendered control of our lives to Him, or we are serving our father the Devil and are surrendering to our own fleshly desires. The former path leads to eternal life and the latter path leads to eternal destruction. The truly wise person will choose life.

MYTH 9:
CHRISTIANITY IS FOR LOSERS

Ned Flanders, a character in *The Simpsons* animated cartoon series, probably typifies the nonbelievers' view of a born-again Christian. Ned keeps plodding along, steadfastly keeping his faith, although all manner of terrible things befall him. In one episode, he loses his business, The Left-Handed Store. In another, the entire town, including his pastor, turns against him when he's falsely accused of being "hepped up on goof balls." On one show, he loses his house, in another his wife, due to the negligence and inconsideration of others. But he keeps giving, turning the other cheek, even surrendering his family's bomb shelter during a "meteor attack." "Poor, dumb old Ned" is the message conveyed by the series. He just seems to keep "beating his head against the wall," all for naught.

Christians who are meek and show a servant's spirit must appear naive, even stupid, to nonbelievers who don't understand the reasons. Media mogul Ted Turner once echoed that world view, calling Christians "bozos," and Christianity a "religion for losers."

Actually, Turner was correct. The New Testament is replete with admonitions for Christians to lose their grip on this life and give up trying to satisfy self, in order to serve others and to instead gain an eternal reward. So in a sense, Christians *are* "losers." So maybe this one is not a myth.

From time to time, it's easy to be discouraged as a follower of Jesus Christ. A Christian believer might even question God's plan, and His sense of fairness, especially when he experiences the "shattered dreams" in life that author Larry Crabb once discussed, in a book by that title.

We know that God shall some day reward us for undergoing persecution as His followers. We also know the meek will inherit the earth in the coming Millennial Kingdom. But what about the here and now? Why do those who try to live a life obedient to God seem to struggle day-to-day to make ends meet; why do they seem to have so much more difficulty than others who have no use for God? Probably all of us at one time or another have looked around at the great fame, fortune, power and easy lifestyles that many evil, ungodly people experience, and we have echoed the cry of the Prophet Jeremiah, "Why does the way of the wicked prosper? Why do all of the faithless live at ease?" It just doesn't seem at all fair! If God is sovereign, then why does He allow such inequity and injustice? Why does He often seem to allow His people to suffer more than those who rebel against Him?

Jesus' words on the subject, at first glance, seem almost to be contradictory. He seems to address the subject from three different angles.

He pretty much answers, up front, the question that's been asked in many books and sermons: "Why do bad things happen to good people?" Jesus tells us, very matter-of-factly, that God "causes His sun to rise on the evil and the good and sends rain on the righteous and the unrighteous." We all live in a fallen, dying, cursed world, meaning that each one of us will suffer, get sick, have loved ones die, experience failures and set-backs, endure hardship and grief, get old and eventually die. Christian and nonbelievers alike experience good and bad periods in their lives, some a different "mix," but none of us have all sunshine and no rain. We all experience severe disappointments. There is no such thing as the *perfect* family, marriage, health, job, church, or life. The same things happen both to good and bad people, Jesus was plainly saying. Believing in Christ gives us no "magic protection."

But elsewhere, the former carpenter invites us, "Come to Me, all you who are heavy, weary and burdened, and I will give you rest. Take My yoke upon you and learn from Me, for I am gentle and humble at heart, and you will find rest for your souls; for My yoke is easy and My burden is light." There, Jesus seems to be telling us that even our earthly lives will be better if we follow Him. He is assuring us that He is not a harsh slave master. He has no desire to abuse us or be mean to us. To the contrary, He said that He came so that we "may have life and have it to the fullest," or "more abundantly." He intends a better life for His followers, not *just* eternal life, as great and wonderful a prize the latter may be.

God is not trying to destroy our fun or to keep us from enjoying life, as many, including myself, have sometimes believed. Just the opposite is true. He wants us to do it "His way," because His wisdom is infinitely greater than ours; He knows that "His way" is better for us in this life and in the next.

Following Christ and gaining eternal life is like uncovering a treasure, Jesus said. It is of infinite value. We cannot measure the value of eternal life by anything here on earth. Gaining even the wealth of the entire world would not come close to the value of acquiring eternal life. And we know God is going to reward each of us in the next life for the good we have done in His name in this life, even the seemingly insignificant good deeds. He promises we will eventually be rewarded many times over what we have lost in this life in order to follow Him, in addition to receiving eternal life. Even giving someone a glass of water in His name will not go unrewarded.

But He promises good things for us in this life, too. "Everything is possible for him who believes," Jesus assures us. He promises to give His children good gifts if we will simply ask Him to do so. Indeed, if we "delight" ourselves in the Lord, He promises to give us "the desires of [our] heart," understanding they must be healthy desires and not outside of His will.

I say "healthy" because great riches and pleasures of this life can choke us spiritually. God knows that very few of us can handle the temptations of always being wealthy and healthy and having everything operate smoothly and perfectly in our lives. So He blesses us by keeping us materially and otherwise dependent upon Him. For, after all, when do we turn to Him, seeking His help and presence — when things are going well for us? No! It's when we are hurting, in need, that we humble ourselves and beg God for His help. We are closest to Him in times of trouble.

Christ tells us not to be anxious about anything. If we follow Him, He'll surely provide all our earthly needs, if not all our cravings. His words on this subject:

> *Therefore I tell you, do not worry about your life, what you will eat; or about your body, what you will wear. Life is more than food, and the body more than clothes.*
>
> *Consider the ravens: they do not sow or reap, they have no store room or barns; yet God feeds them. And how much more valuable you are than birds! Who of you by worrying can add a single hour to his life? Since you cannot do this very little thing, why do you worry about the rest?*
>
> *Consider how the lilies grow. They do not labor or spin. Yet I tell you, not even Solomon in all his splendor was dressed like one of these. If that is how God clothes the grass of the field, which is here today, and tomorrow is thrown into the fire, how much more will He clothe you, O you of little faith! And do not set your heart on what you will eat or drink; do not worry about it. For the pagan world runs after all such things, and your Father knows*

that you need them. But seek His kingdom, and all these things will be given to you as well.

If we are generous to others, God promises He'll generously reward us. "Give, and it will be given to you. A good measure, pressed down, shaken together and running over, will be poured into your lap. For with the measure you use, it will be measured to you." In my half century on this planet, I can agree with King David, "I was young and now I am old, yet I have never seen the righteous forsaken or their children begging bread." God will take care of our material needs if we put Him first.

Living the Christian life can reduce anxiety beyond simply taking away the fear of death and giving us peace of mind, which is valuable in itself. It can reduce the day-to-day anxieties associated with doing wrong and getting caught, or suffering the consequences of our wrong. Andy Stanley compares it to driving within the speed limit — if we do so, we need not be constantly watching, nervously, for a law enforcement officer. And if we're living an obedient Christian life, we no longer need to worry about a lot of things that disturb the sleep of other people. For example, we probably won't need to worry about getting fired for embezzlement, getting caught by a jealous husband or wife, being jailed for drunk driving, being busted by the IRS for tax fraud, or developing health problems from abusing our bodies with drugs or alcohol or engaging in dangerous sexual liaisons. A clear conscience doesn't guarantee a problem-free life, but it can reduce a lot of stress. Mental health professionals agree that getting rid of guilt is very helpful to one's emotional state. True Christians can do that, knowing their sins are forgiven and that they remain blameless before God.

Again, God is a good parent; He does not want us to hurt ourselves or others. By living a life consistent with His Word and praying for guidance, believers can possess a discerning spirit, enabling them to know what path is prudent in almost every circumstance. In short, being a Christian can improve our quality of life. In the "here and now," there are many advantages to being in right standing with God and having a good relationship with those around us.

TAKE UP YOUR CROSS

From another perspective, however, we find Jesus predicting that His true followers will face great pain, hardship, sadness, abandonment and difficulty in this earthly life.

Anyone who "does not carry his cross and follow Me cannot be My disciple," Jesus warned. We must "deny ourselves" to follow Jesus, He demanded. In fact, we must love and obey Him so much that, in comparison, we should hate our families, even our own lives!

Jesus undoubtedly said this because He knew that many of His followers would have to make that very difficult choice: following Him, even at the cost of losing family and friends, versus abandoning Him in order to keep peace in this life with them. "Do you think I came to bring peace on earth?" Jesus asked, "No, I tell you, but division. From now on there will be five in one family divided against each other — three against two and two against three. They will be divided, father against son and son against father, mother against daughter and daughter against mother, mother-in-law against daughter-in-law and daughter-in-law against mother-in-law." A Christian might even have to end a dating relationship in order to please Christ, as heart-rending as that severance can be. Or he might have to quit a lucrative vocation that had forced him to compromise principles and act against God's will.

The End Times will be particularly difficult for believers, Jesus predicted. "Brother will betray brother to death, and a father his child. Children will rebel against their parents and have them put to death. All men will hate you because of me...." Believers will be persecuted, insulted and slandered for following Him, He promises. He predicted that His followers would be flogged, arrested, betrayed by family, hated, persecuted and killed.

We know that the early Church was persecuted harshly by the Romans. It is believed that all the apostles were martyred. But did you know that as many Christians have been martyred throughout the world in the past generation as were killed in the entire prior nineteen-hundred-year period of Christianity? Indeed, persecution still exists in many forms, including death for belief in Jesus Christ.

Paul writes that our struggle is not against human beings, but against the demonic powers and forces that control these people. A Christian may be puzzled when a friend turns against him for no apparent reason, a teacher gives her a difficult time or an undeserved poor grade, an employer passes over him for a promotion when his performance has been better than others, or she finds herself ostracized from a group. None of these things may make any earthly sense whatsoever, but Paul is saying that the Christian need not be baffled or discouraged, understanding that these things are being done to the believer because his antagonist is being controlled by his father the Devil. Jesus often warned that if they hated Him, they most certainly will hate those of us who follow Him. "A student is not above his teacher," He explained.

As a teen, I remember a verse of a song in church, "No, no, it's not an easy way," and thinking, "This Christian life is probably far too tough for me to handle!"

COUNT THE COST

In fact, Jesus warns us not to even bother pursuing Him until and unless we have considered what this Christian life is going to entail and whether we are truly committed — dedicated enough to follow through with it. "Suppose one of you wants to build a tower. Will he not first sit down and estimate the cost to see if he has enough money to complete it?" Jesus asked. "For if he lays the foundation and is not able to finish it, everyone who sees it will ridicule him, saying, 'This fellow began to build and was not able to finish.' Or suppose a king is about to go to war with another king. Will he not first sit down and consider whether he is able with 10,000 men to oppose the one coming against him with 20,000? If he is not able, he will send a delegation while the other is still a long way off and will ask for terms of peace. In the same way, any of you who does not give up everything he has cannot be My disciple." Jesus will give us His Holy Spirit to help us and comfort us along the way. But He does not want us to start the Christian life and then abandon it, giving up on Him. He wants us to be fully committed, for our entire lifetime; Christianity is not a frivolous or temporary endeavor. "No one who puts his hand to the plow and looks back is fit for service in the kingdom of God," Jesus told a potential disciple.

WRONG MOTIVE!

It seems clear that Jesus did not want people following Him just so that their earthly life would be easier. There was no promise of "follow Me and you'll get rich." He ceased the miracle of multiplying loaves and fish after doing it twice, for example, because the crowds were gathering for the wrong reason, simply wanting to be fed. We're to follow Him because we *love* Him, because we thirst after righteousness and truly desire to commune with, please and obey Him, and want to live with Him eternally. He does not want us pursuing Christianity because of the present comfort or material benefit we think such a relationship might afford.

It could be compared to choosing a spouse. Would we want someone to marry us just because we make a good income and could provide for him or her exceptionally well? Or would we prefer a husband or wife who is marrying us because he or she is attracted to us, enjoys being with us, wants to share our lives, and loves us for who we are? It's the same with Jesus. He wants us to have the right motive.

One wonders how many people have given up on Christ when their hopes and desires have been dashed: when a loved one dies, when a child or spouse walks away forever, when a business deal collapses or a job is lost, or when the doctor says the dreaded word "cancer." Or when they finally realize that they were not going to always going to be healthy and prosperous, as many false teachers have promised with their popular "health and wealth" doctrine. Why, if some of these false teachers were correct, we would *never* die if we just possessed enough faith and gave them enough money. We would remain healthy and rich forever!

Indeed, as a believer matures in his walk with Christ, he often finds that God increasingly tests his faith, constantly refining it. And how does He do that? By bringing trials, resistance, trauma, or problems in life which seem to have no solution. Usually, when you find a strong, devoted follower of Jesus Christ, you will discover he or she has experienced a lifetime of great personal difficulties, sad occurrences, defeats and set-backs. Like a muscle, our faith is strengthened by being exercised. If you want to draw closer to God, be ready to suffer, because that is His favorite way to "grow us up." He often brings out the best in us in seemingly mysterious ways — certainly unpleasant ones, at times. But He promises not to push us beyond our limit.

IT'S ALL GOOD!

So we see that the three seemingly contradictory predictions about the effects of living an obedient Christian life are not contradictory at all. Christians do share the "rain and sunshine" experience with unbelievers; there is no difference in many things that they face in life. Christians can reasonably expect persecution as they follow Christ, along with lots of trials, tough experiences, and difficulties. And yet they are promised help, strength, and provision by Christ — if they keep Him first in their lives.

Here is a concept I have fully grasped only in recent years: as Paul wrote, God works in *all* things to the benefit of those who love Him and who are called according to His purpose — even the "bad" things that happen to us. We learn from the tragic and difficult occurrences in our lives. Our faith becomes stronger. We learn to endure and depend upon Him fully. Our faith during such trials serves as an example to other Christians, and a witness to nonbelievers, that serving Jesus is a genuine experience, not something contrived or imaginary. Perhaps nothing speaks of faith more positively and strongly than endurance of trials.

And, returning to the question Jeremiah raised about the wicked who seemed to always have such an unfair amount of success in his life, consider what Jesus has said about these people:

> *But woe to you who are rich,*
> *for you have already received your comfort.*
> *Woe to you who are well fed now,*
> *for you will go hungry.*
>
> *Woe to you who laugh now,*
> *for you will mourn and weep.*
> *Woe to you when all men speak well of you,*
> *for that is how their fathers treated the false prophets.*

In other words, the bad guys' time eventually will come. We are witnessing only an extremely small slice of time in our life here on earth. Compared to eternity, it is virtually nothing. Every man and woman will be judged and God will dispense perfect justice, far better than anyone in a black robe could do. Eventually, God's people will get their just reward and His enemies will receive their just punishment. This wealth, power and ease that we see some of God's enemies enjoying now will dim quite insignificantly in comparison to the rewards and treasures to be received by those who diligently seek God and His righteousness. The story will end perfectly and correctly. Christians simply need to continue being "losers," knowing that ultimately they will be the greatest winners by far.

MYTH 10:
CHRISTIANITY ISN'T FAIR

I have some friends who use their minds as well as their emotions when it comes to Christian issues. They like to think about it, even challenge long-held assumptions. There's nothing wrong with that; it's even commendable. Isn't it a good idea to use our brains as well as our hearts when making purchases, choosing a mate, deciding on a career, and in making life's other major decisions? So it certainly is appropriate to consider, on an intellectual basis, a potential eternal relationship with Jesus Christ and not just jump into it because our emotions have been touched. God provided us with logic and reasoning abilities, and I don't think He's offended when we ask tough questions or even ponder the unanswerable.

Inevitably, one of the toughest, and most common, questions relates to the "fairness issue." How can a loving God send people to an eternal Hell if they've had no opportunity to ever hear about Jesus Christ and His gift of salvation through the cross? "Is it fair," they ask, "that God would forever punish people who have lived all of their lives deep in a jungle of Africa or South America, or in some communist, Muslim or Hindu nation, who have never had an opportunity to hear the Gospel, or have received only a partial or distorted message of Jesus Christ?" Or how about young children or the mentally impaired? Are they held accountable for not making such a decision?

We know that, before Jesus, Jews were saved through their faith in Jehovah, which they demonstrated through their sacrificial system and in their attempts to keep the Law given to Moses. Until the prophets, they didn't even know a Messiah was coming and even then had a veiled picture of Him, at that. Jesus' perfect sacrifice was in the future for them, as it is in the past for us, but served them just the same, even though God's full plan of redemption had not yet been revealed.

But many have asked, was even that system fair? Was it fair that one had to become a circumcised Jew in order to please God the Creator? And what about the millions of souls throughout the world during those thousands of years, who knew nothing about Moses, sacrifice, the Law, or had never even met a Jew? How could it be fair for God to send those people to Hell, having lived their entire lives in ignorance of His plan — especially those who'd lived moral, decent lives?

To our way of thinking, none of it seems fair at all. We can't fathom a loving deity who would treat His creation in such a manner. And many people have used this "fairness issue" as an excuse to refuse acceptance of Christ. "He may or may not be the Son of God, but I can't accept Christianity because it isn't fair!"

Do We Have a Valid Excuse?

But today, with the explosive growth of the communication media, fewer and fewer people can allege that they have never had a chance to hear the Gospel. Shortwave radio penetrates nearly every nook and cranny of our globe and, if you have ever listened to it, those airwaves are full of Christian broadcasting of different varieties. Hundreds of millions of Bibles have circulated to every nation, with translations in almost every language. Missionaries have traveled to every nation, even to small, distant tribes, to proclaim Christ. Television, the Internet, radio, pamphlets and other means of communication are making the Gospel accessible to just about everyone who wants to hear it.

We who live in Western society cannot even pretend that we have been deprived of hearing God's truth. Church doors are open several days a week in most areas, there are Christian bookstores in most towns, and religious broadcasting is available "24/7." Believers witness to unbelievers, sometimes offering Gospel tracts on the streets or in the hospitals and other public places. The Good News is proclaimed all around us. We'd have to be deaf and blind to avoid hearing the Gospel message several times during our lifetime; we are bombarded with it.

Jesus makes it clear that accessibility to His message gives us responsibility to either accept or reject it. If we ignore the Gospel, we are effectively rejecting Christ. Remember the story He told of the rich man in Hell? When the rich man begged Abraham to send Lazarus to warn his five living brothers, Abraham replied, "They have Moses and the prophets; let them listen to them." Similarly, anyone who stands at the Judgment who lived in Western culture will likely hear, "You had an abundance of Christian preachers and teachers. Why didn't you listen to them?" We Americans, at least, have no excuse.

A SECOND CHANCE?

Many cite Hebrews 9:27, which notes that we only die once and, after that, face judgment. Or, "Salvation is found in no one else [than Jesus Christ], for there is no other name under Heaven given to man by which we must be saved." They contend that these verses prove that no one — even those who have never heard the Gospel — escapes Hell unless he repents and puts his trust in Jesus Christ.

How a person can believe without ever hearing the Gospel, they do not explain. Indeed, Paul addressed that very issue. He wrote to the Romans, "How, then, can they call on the One they have not believed in? And how can they believe in the One of whom they have not heard? And how can they hear without someone preaching to them?" Paul felt an urgency to get the Gospel to everyone.

I personally think that a person who never hears (and, therefore, never accepts) the Gospel dies unsaved, facing some type of separation from God forever. But I can't be dogmatic about that position.

No one has ever adequately explained to me what Peter was talking about when he wrote that Jesus "preached to the spirits in prison who disobeyed long ago when God waited patiently in the days of Noah when the Ark was being built." Peter had almost surely heard this revelation from the risen Lord. Was Jesus giving unbelievers who had died a second chance to accept God's plan of salvation? If not, why then was he preaching to them? This remains a mystery. It may be a minority view among Bible believers, but I do not believe that we can completely rule out that He was giving them an opportunity to repent and to cease their rebellion against God.

Without sounding heretical, we simply do not know for sure what happens to the departed souls of those who have never had an opportunity to hear the Gospel. The Bible does not address the question directly. As Billy Graham has suggested, God may be more gracious than some people think He is. Paul suggested as much, telling an intellectual audience in Athens, "In the past God overlooked...ignorance."

The God in whom I believe is just and fair and, even more importantly, He is sovereign. He can save anyone He chooses to save. As Jesus said, "With God all things are possible." We should not make arrogant assumptions. He has not chosen to disclose everything to us. I have difficulty imagining God severely punishing one who's never heard the Gospel, don't you?

The Bible makes no mention of reincarnation and certainly not Purgatory, but it does indicate that God will not ignore those who sincerely pursue Him. There have been innumerable cases in which people in pagan cultures have recognized that there is one God, the Creator, and who have tried to live righteously and seek His will. And in those situations, God seems to provide someone or some means to present the Gospel to those who diligently seek Him. Cornelius, the Roman centurion, was an early example. In Acts, Chapter 10, we read that God sent Peter to his house to preach to him the Gospel because he was attempting to live righteously and was generous to the poor. Cornelius and his household were converted and baptized as the result of Peter being sent to him. His search was rewarded.

DEGREES OF PUNISHMENT?

Upon several occasions, Jesus inferred that there will not only be degrees of reward, based on what believers have done with their gifts and abilities in this life, but also degrees of punishment for those who are lost. For example, Jesus told His disciples that, if they preached the Gospel in a town where it was rejected, "I tell you the truth, it will be more bearable for Sodom and Gomorrah on the day of judgment than for that town." And to the residents of Kurazin and Bethsaida in which He performed miracles but was rejected, Jesus warned, "But I tell you, it will be more bearable for Tyre and Sidon on the day of judgment than for you." Tyre, Sidon, Sodom and Gomorrah were pagan, wicked cities documented in the Old Testament and considered to be the ultimate "sin cities" in that day. Jesus was explaining that judgment for unbelievers will be far more severe among those who have heard the Gospel and rejected it, than for those who have never heard it.

For hundreds of years, most Christian scholars have been willing to concede that children, at least until a certain "age of accountability," are saved when they die. Jesus' comments seem to support that notion. He disclosed that children have angels who appear on their behalf before God in Heaven. And He requires that we all become as little children to enter the Kingdom of Heaven, noting that His Kingdom is going to be inhabited by those similar to little children. So we can be pretty confident that there is at least one exception — children — and by logical extension — the mentally challenged. (Do you realize this implies that the souls of tens of millions of aborted babies are populating Heaven today?)

To push the argument further, it is possible that, for those who have never heard of God's way of salvation in ancient or modern times, there will be little or no punishment. Or perhaps they will be given that opportunity at a future time. We just do not know the exact nature of His plan.

HE DOES THE CHOOSING

But one must also consider that our human sense of fairness may not match God's perfect sense of fairness. After all, He is the Creator; He can choose whomever He wishes and reject those He desires to reject.

Indeed, in His ideal creation, illustrated in the Garden of Eden, *all* were chosen by God. It was a supremely "fair" system. However, it was our sin and rebellion that separated us from Him. And to this day, the great majority choose to rebel against God. It is not that they don't know about a Supreme God, Creator of the universe, it is rather that they make a conscious choice to neglect Him and His offer of salvation.

This issue of "fairness" apparently was raised early in the Church, because even Paul mentions it. Using an Old Testament illustration, Paul noted that, even before they were born, before they had done anything good or bad, God chose Jacob and rejected Esau. Likewise, God has a "purpose in election" that we should not question, Paul warns. Drawing from passages in Isaiah, he writes:

> *But who are you, O man, to talk back to God?*
> *"Shall what is formed say to Him who formed it,*
> *'Why did you make me like this?'" Does not the potter have the right to make out of the same lump of clay some pottery for noble purposes and some for common use?*

> *What if God, choosing to show His wrath and make His power known, bore with great patience the objects of His wrath — prepared for destruction? What if He did this to make riches of His glory known to the objects of His mercy, whom He prepared in advance for glory — even us, whom He also called, not only from the Jews, but also from the Gentiles?*

You might even say that one of the means by which an all-knowing, all-powerful God chooses some and rejects others is by allowing certain people to be born into nations and at times in which the Gospel has been available, even into homes with influential Christian parents, family or friends. For, as Paul told the Atheneans, God determines the times and exact places where we all will live on this earth; it is not just by luck or chance that we have been positioned to be exposed to the Gospel. We who have heard it should be very grateful to God, since it is not by accident that we have been blessed with that opportunity. And those who are being chosen are in a distinct minority; many are called but few are chosen, Jesus said. It is a supreme privilege!

If we reject it, with the wealth of information we have, then we have no one to blame but ourselves. I anticipate no "second chance" after I am dead, that's for sure. And those of us who think we are Christians should constantly test and examine ourselves to be certain that we are in the faith, proving it to ourselves and to others by holy living.

So our position should not be one in which God's "fairness" is questioned. As Paul writes, who are we, with our finite knowledge, to challenge the fairness of the infinite Creator? *We must simply trust that He is a good and just God and will ultimately dispense perfect justice for all of humankind.* We should accept that although none of us "rebels" deserve His grace, kindness and mercy, He chose to pour it out upon some of us by convicting us of our sins and calling us to Himself to become His sons and daughters, to eventually reign with Him. Again, we should be immensely grateful for that opportunity, and we should pursue Him and His ways with all of our might, in humble thanksgiving.

THE REAL ISSUE

The only real issue then, is not whether it's fair but, rather, whether the Gospel message is *true*. If we acknowledge that Christ is the Son of God who died for our sins, then we should accept Him. The decision as to whether the Gospel is true has no direct correlation with the "fairness" issue. Something can be true but, at the same time, "unfair," and vice versa.

We should leave "fairness" up to God. It's not a valid excuse to worry about how He's going to treat the other guy. Be concerned about our own relationship with Him, our own eternal destiny. Like a student in school, we should attend to our own homework and let the teacher deal with the errant classmate.

And if we do accept Jesus Christ, then it is our duty to help spread the Gospel throughout the world, by our direct efforts and by funding, facilitating and praying for preachers, teachers and missionaries who are attempting to communicate Christ's message to everyone in the world.

When we stand before our Judge someday, I do not believe that any of us will be able to truthfully say that He was unfair to us or anyone else. Indeed, if He rendered justice, instead of mercy, none of us would be saved, right? None of us is righteous enough in himself to deserve to reign with Christ eternally. Only by His grace are we saved, through faith. It is the gift of God through Christ Jesus our Lord. Let us be thankful and give Him praise for such a wonderful gift.

MYTH 11:
CHRISTIANS AREN'T SUPPOSED TO HAVE FUN

I'm sure I wasn't the only one growing up in a legalistic church who thought God's favorite word was "No." The hellfire and brimstone sermons we frequently heard, especially in "revival services," seemed to be full of condemnation. There were so many rules, most of which appeared to be designed to prevent any pleasure or enjoyment in life. The God they depicted seemed eager to cast us into Hell. He was portrayed as angry, demanding, and short of patience, and there was almost no talk of His grace. It wasn't considered a powerful sermon if it didn't scare you to death.

Their entire presentation of the Gospel seemed to be in the negative. As a law school classmate of mine (who'd come from the same religious background) and I later discussed, even the "testimonies" of the faithful were presented in the negative: "I don't smoke, drink or curse anymore. . ." It was all about "not doing stuff" and "keeping the rules." And, of course, many people are quite comfortable with having a set of rules; that way they don't have to think for themselves or study the Bible to determine what God really demands of us. They want the pastor to give them a set of rules.

Many of us fled those churches at first opportunity. In fact, I darkened a church door only a few times for a period of about 15 years, beginning in my college days. I tried to say to myself that it was because I was angry at God, didn't trust Him, maybe didn't even like Him anymore. After all, He'd allowed my family to suffer enormous grief and trials when a loved one died, which triggered a chain of very difficult events.

But the real reason for my departure was that I knew I simply could not keep all of those "rules." Going to church, hearing those harsh sermons, and being with people whom I then (erroneously) thought had "their act together," made me uncomfortable.

Strangely, those dear folk admitted that it was by God's grace that we are saved, without any good works, a gift from Him, but for some reason taught that it required holy living, keeping the "rules" (God's Law), to *remain* saved and stay within the boundaries of God's love. Despite all that the New Testament says about our efforts not saving us, they just couldn't get away from "works." And I was honest enough with myself to know that I could not live a perfect, sin-free life as they demanded, and decided I wasn't going to be hypocritical.

Sadly, like millions of others, I had yet not been introduced to the true God of the Bible. And I misunderstood what He requires of us and why He requires it.

It's Not About Rules

Opposite of what many think, the Bible doesn't depict God as being "into rules." And those "rules" that He does ordain, I eventually learned, are for our own good, to protect us and to provide order in a fallen, sinful world.

Ideally, in a perfect world, there would be no rules at all. We wouldn't need any. We would share and get along nicely with others, loving them as we love ourselves. We would forgive and defer to each other, competing to see who could be more generous, kind and helpful. We'd all have everything we needed and wanted. There would be no ego contests and no war.

But, as we know quite well, we live in a world which is far from perfect. And it would be pure chaos and anarchy if we did not have a set of rules by which to live, just as automobiles in a city need "rules" — road signs, traffic lights, painted boundary lines, etc. — to prevent collisions.

And if we are going to search for a set of rules or principles by which we can live, why not try to determine what the Creator has given us, since He designed us, has been around for quite a long time and knows a bit more than we do?

If you consider the story of Adam and Eve, initially there was only *one* rule. Everything was permissible in the Garden of Eden, with one exception. God told them that they were not allowed to eat "from the Tree of Knowledge of Good and Evil, for when you eat of it you will surely die." And yet they could not keep even that one rule. Through that act of disobedience, the Bible teaches, the parents of the human race brought sin, death, destruction and suffering upon all creation.

Then for a long period of time — for at least hundreds, if not thousands, of years — there was no law given by God to humankind. The Jewish nation was started through Abraham's faith, but no law was given until much later, under Moses, after the children of Israel had been liberated from Egyptian slavery. There were periods of time, in fact, during which "everyone did as He saw fit."

And, although thousands of criminal and civil laws and kosher rules found in the Old Testament and elsewhere in the Jewish law were blessed by God, remember that Jehovah Himself restricted the Commandments he gave Moses to ten simple, basic ones. But His chosen people proved, time and again, that they couldn't and wouldn't keep even those basic Ten Commandments.

When He came, Jesus spoke a lot about what is right and wrong. He reaffirmed, at one point or another, all of the

Commandments, except the fourth one, regarding keeping the Sabbath. Jesus distilled all of the Law into two commandments: "Love the Lord your God with all your heart and with all your soul and with all your mind," and, "Love your neighbor as yourself." He explained, "All of the Law and Prophets hang on these two commandments."

On many occasions Jesus strongly inferred that the Pharisees and other Jewish leaders had gone much too far, throughout the years, in adding to the "rules" which had been imposed upon the Jewish people, that they had become much too burdensome. In fact, Jesus said, "They tie up heavy loads and put them on men's shoulders, but they themselves are not willing to lift a finger to move them." He criticized these "traditions" of men.

The first Church didn't have a lot of rules. Former Pharisee (and a fanatical keeper of the law), Paul wrote, "Everything is permissible for me — but not everything is beneficial. Everything is permissible for me — but I will not be mastered by anything." Indeed, the theme of many Paul's letters to the early churches was the freedom we have in Christ and explaining that the Law cannot save us.

That is not to say that the first Church did not have difficulty with the transition from a religion of "rules" to a religion of "grace." Peter, arguably the leader of the first Church, had a very difficult time breaking free from the laws and traditions in which he had been raised since birth. It was not until he had a vision from God on three occasions that he was convinced that all things are now "kosher," and began teaching that concept to the Church.

Even so, the Church elders had to meet in Jerusalem to resolve, once and for all, whether the Jewish law was to be imposed upon non-Jewish believers. Although he had continued to honor Jewish law and traditions so as not to offend potential converts or weaker believers, it appears that during that important meeting the apostle Paul did not want any "law" for Christians. He forcefully argued, "Now then, why do you try to test God by putting on the necks of the disciples a yoke that neither we nor our fathers have been able to bear? No! We believe it is through the grace of our Lord Jesus that we are saved, just as we are." Christ had fulfilled the whole Law, so that we who trust in Him for our salvation also fulfill it.

Those Church forefathers reached a compromise wherein only four "rules" were adopted for the Church. Believers were to abstain from eating food which had been offered to idols, from ingesting blood, from eating animals which had been strangled, and from sexual immorality. To the Christians at Corinth, Paul even downplayed the "food offered to idols" rule, but agreed that they should not eat such food if it would offend another believer.

One might argue, however, that the New Testament is full of "rules." For example, Paul writes that adulterers, the sexually immoral, homosexuals, thieves, greedy people, drunkards, slanderers and robbers will not "inherit the Kingdom of God." In his letter to Timothy, Paul added to his list "kidnappers, liars, murderers, those who attack their parents, those who curse and swear, and those who are generally rebellious toward God." He added, "We know that the law is good if one uses it properly." And Jesus told the apostle John that those who are unfaithful to Him, the corrupt, the immoral, idol worshipers, murderers, those who communicate with demons, and "all liars" will experience the "second death," spending eternity in the Lake of Fire.

You can call those "rules," but Jesus, John and Paul were saying in essence, "People who continue to practice such sins are not Christians. They are demonstrating whom they belong to, by their evil deeds and lifestyles." Some true Christians may slip back into sinful behavior from time to time, but it is not an ongoing lifestyle, as before they were converted.

Paul did set forth some rules for church officers and leaders. For example, he required that elders (or pastors) of his churches abstain from alcohol, have only one wife, not be a lover of money, and have a well-behaved family, so that he would be a good example to the community. To the deacons, he demanded much of the same, with one exception: a deacon must not be a heavy drinker, Paul wrote. And he outlined his recommendations for holy living to parents, teachers, to young people, actually to all believers, throughout the discourse of his letters to the churches. He admitted that living a godly life is not an easy matter. But Paul never advocated an imposition of the Jewish Law upon Gentile believers. To the contrary, he resisted the "Judaizers" (who required adherence to the Law) through the duration of his ministry.

It's About Relationship

The fact of the matter is, whether it's many or few rules that God gives us, we've all proven through the centuries that we cannot keep them, at least to His supremely high standards. But since the penalty for sin is death, God had to do something for us, if any are to be saved.

That's why He gave His Son to die for our sins, to pay the penalty in full for our breach of God's "rules." Jesus explained that He fulfilled God's Law by His sacrificial death. He died in our place. He doesn't "dumb down" God's law, or nullify it. He says that if you trust fully in Him, you are no longer condemnable. It is as if we have kept God's entire Law, from birth to death. We are clothed in His righteousness, since we have none of our own and cannot fully keep the Law.

Wrapped in that cloak of righteousness, Paul assures us, "Therefore, there is now no condemnation for those who are in Christ Jesus, because through Christ Jesus the law of the spirit of life set me free from the law of sin and death." He adds, "For what the law was powerless to do in that it was weakened by the sinful nature [or flesh], God did by sending His own Son in the likeness of sinful man to be a sin offering. And so He condemned sin in sinful man [or, in the flesh] in order that the righteous requirements of the law might be fully met in us, who do not live according to the sinful nature, but according to the Spirit."

In fact, Paul explained that God knew we would never be able to keep His Law. Instead, the Law actually was established to illustrate how "off the mark" we are in meeting His high and holy standards, *driving us to Him* after we have recognized how sinful we are. So, when asked what work God requires of us, Jesus replied very simply, "The work of God is this: to believe in the One He has sent [Jesus]." That is all we can do to meet God's high standard.

Jesus was the only One, according to the Bible, with whom God was "well pleased." So only He was available, throughout the history of humankind, to serve as the perfect sacrifice on our behalf. No other sacrifice, man or beast, was worthy.

And why did God want to give His Son as a sacrifice to make us righteous? Because He wants a *relationship* with us. He wants to be a friend to those He has created, who have a free will, humans who can decide whether or not they want to be His friend. He does not desire just a people dutifully laboring to keep His "rules," don't you see?

Relationship was what God was seeking when He met Adam and Eve each day in the garden, in the cool of the evening. It was a relationship God sought with Abraham, Moses and the chosen children of Israel throughout the centuries. It was a new, personal, trusting, non-fearful, intimate relationship with God the Father that Jesus offered. And that's what He seeks with you and me. (After all, He doesn't need anything else we have to offer. He can accomplish His will without our puny efforts.)

Jesus gave us a "new commandment" which proves it's about relationship, not rules. "A new command I give you: Love one another. As I have loved, so you must love one another. By this all men will know that you are My disciples, if you love one another." Jesus wants to restore the original intention of love, friendship, trust, intimacy, and communication with God and our fellow-believers. That has been His ideal, since creation.

Throughout life — at home, in school, at work — we learn that we are rewarded for good deeds and hard work and suffer penalties for poor performance (positive and negative reinforcement, as mentioned previously). That seems to be the norm. But Christ offers this new, totally different method, whereby He accepts upon Himself the penalty for our failed performance so that our relationship with God can be restored.

Interestingly, when we as believers fully understand that Jesus has taken our condemnation upon Himself and that all our sins — past, present and future — are covered by His blood, it has an opposite effect of what might be expected. Instead of wanting to sin more, it drives us toward a lifestyle which is more holy. We can serve and forgive others, as He has forgiven us. We want to please God instead of ourselves. We become thankful for what He has done for us.

As we grow in that relationship, allowing the Holy Spirit to take more and more control of our lives, we discover that "keeping the rules" becomes secondary because our minds have now become "renewed." We become new "creations" in Christ. We find ourselves more easily conforming to those limits God has given us which permit a peaceful, orderly and productive life. Although we are always tempted until the day we die, we develop more "self-control" through the guidance and restraint of the Holy Spirit living within us.

And then we find that, as James predicted, the closer we get to God, the closer He comes to us. He begins to reveal Himself to us, lets us view the world as He does, gives us wisdom we never had before, and provides us with joy and contentment of a personal relationship with Himself. We can draw close to God through obedience to His commandments, studying His Word, communing with Him in meditation and prayer, and through fellowship with our brothers and sisters in Christ.

So the God I've come to know as an adult is a "Yes" God. He's positive, not negative. He is into freedom. He's not wanting to throw lightning bolts when we mess up, even though we deserve it. He's not trying to keep us away from Himself; the opposite is true. He's allowing us latitude within the love and safety of a relationship with Him, in a lifestyle of freedom and peace that only He can offer.

And, again, we begin to realize that the few "rules" that God does impose upon us are for our own good. They are given not to punish us, deny our fun or to make life difficult. Rather, they are given because He loves us. Because He's infinite and has been around forever, God — the perfect loving Parent — knows what is best for us and what can harm us in the short or long term. He will give us guidance and wisdom in all situations, if we merely ask. His will is easy to discover and comply with, just by reading His written Word.

SIN STEALS FREEDOM

If Christians sometimes seem judgmental or "anti-fun," it might be that they are now viewing the world more the way that God sees it. What offends God should offend His children. They should view some things that the world considers "fun" as dangerous to body and soul.

Ironically, it is not God who robs us of our freedom in this world. Ultimately, it is *sin* which does the most to eventually steal our freedom. After you have lived a few decades and observed the patterns of life, you can more fully understand and appreciate that God's "rules" just make common sense. Taking care of your body generally translates to better health and a longer life, for example. One man, one woman, married for life, is ideal for many good reasons. Properly guiding, directing and restricting one's children generally translates to better adjusted, more successful futures for them. Most of these "rules" God gives to us are illustrated by the "sowing and reaping" principle of the Bible. If we sow good seed, we generally reap good fruit. Bad seed, bad fruit. Years later, we harvest what we earlier have planted in our lives.

When Satan tempted Eve, his line of attack was to make her feel that she was missing out on something better for her life, that God's Word could not be trusted, and that He was trying to hide or withhold something good from her. He lied about God's character.

Although he doesn't masquerade in the form of a serpent today, that is still Satan's way of tempting everyone. He continues to persuade, through dazzling advertisements, the entertainment media, peer pressure, and especially by appealing to our lusts, ego, covetousness, insecurities and greed. He tells us that we can be totally free without parameters for our lives. He keeps telling us that God doesn't exist or, if He does, He is not serious, that He is not telling us the truth. He'd have us believe that the Bible is only a bunch of irrelevant myths. Satan tries to deceive us into thinking there are no positive benefits in this nonsensical, sissy Christianity stuff. And he really wants to convince us that there is no Hell, that there are no consequences in this or the next life for our rebellion against God. Satan discounts Jesus' promise that He came to give us a more abundant life. He wants us to disregard Jesus' warnings that Satan is a murderer and the father of all lies. Yet millions of people — the great majority — fall prey to his lies. He is still the "great deceiver."

Just as Adam and Eve lost their freedom, instead of gaining freedom by rebelling against God and breaking His one rule, we lose our freedom when we step outside God's gracious boundaries. Sin entangles us and robs us.

As a teenager, I observed my non-Christian classmates as they were entering into adulthood, sampling and experimenting with all sorts of sin. At times, it felt so uncool not to be following them. But as the author of Proverbs writes, "There is a way that seems right to a man, but in the end it leads to death." As I have reached middle age, I see that many of those people are now reaping what they had sown in those early years. Some became workaholics, dominated by out-of-control and unsatisfied greed. Many had unwanted pregnancies, abortions, sexually transmitted diseases and broken marriages. Several had serious tobacco, alcohol, sexual and drug addictions. Others developed severe health problems and even died at a young age because of wrong choices. Many experienced depression and anxiety as the result of their actions. Yet others have suffered a loss of self-respect, become dependent on others, or lost opportunities and experienced unnecessary poverty, jail time, even death, as the result of their sin. In the end, sin caused them to lose their freedom, and they are now in bondage as the result of participation in activities which initially seemed so exciting, glamorous, or cool.

Each generation thinks it's discovered a new, smarter, more exciting way to live. But undoubtedly, Satan sits back and laughs, as he knows he's deceived the masses throughout the centuries into making the same, stupid mistakes. Our world culture is dominated by Satan. He is the ruler of this present world system, according to Jesus. He blinds most people from seeing that the beginning of a sinful path — which admittedly can be quite attractive and tempting — eventually leads to destruction and death.

Like the caring parent that He is, God does not want us to suffer the consequences of following those wrong paths. That is why He graciously and lovingly provides us with some limited "rules" by which to live. And in the long run — certainly, in the *eternal* long run — it is much, much easier, much more liberating, to live within those rules than to rebel against them.

One learns that maximum freedom is actually found under God's authority, just the opposite of what Satan and the world's culture tries to deceive us into believing. Bottom line: living for Christ is more fun and better all the way around, as anyone who's done it both ways will testify.

MYTH 12:
THE BIBLE TEACHES THIS WORLD IS COMING TO AN END

Even if they don't accept Bible prophecies regarding coming events as being accurate or literal predictions of the future, most people will admit that they are not very optimistic about the long-term prospects for life on this planet.

Society, and sometimes the environment itself, seems to be rapidly veering off toward some disastrous course. The realistic prospect of all-out nuclear war looms on the horizon. Increasing terrorism, war and crime threaten the hope for peace and security. Other problems, too, seem to be getting worse instead of better, even though scientific advances attempt to stay ahead of them. Population overgrowth occurs in areas which can least afford it; famines and dire poverty are constant threats. Pollution threatens our water, land and atmosphere, likely contributing to an increase of cancer and other disease, among other consequences. Incurable diseases like AIDS threaten entire continents, as new ones come on the scene.

Statistics prove that natural disasters and storms are on the increase. There has been a dramatic increase in earthquakes worldwide, for example. In the 1940s there were just 51 earthquakes measuring above 6.0 on the Richter Scale; in the 1950s, 475; in the 1980s, 1,085; and in the 1990s, 1,514.

Many things have occurred during the past generation in fulfillment of Biblical prophecy. Against all odds, millions of Jewish people, who had been dispersed into over 120 nations, failed to assimilate into those cultures and have instead returned by the millions to the land of Israel in the past several decades, a repopulation unprecedented in history.

There are other conditions described by the prophet Daniel 2,500 years ago with regard to the end of this era; for example, that "travel and education shall be vastly increased." Cults and counterfeit spirituality are everywhere, fulfilling Matthew 24:24. Increased psychic phenomena, spiritualism, satanic worship, witchcraft, nature worship and the New Age movement fulfill the prophecies in I Timothy 4:1. We see the beginnings of a New World Order, with a united Europe and global economy, as prophesied in the Old and New Testament.

We see an alarming increase in apostasy in the Church as predicted by Paul. He wrote that all creation groans and labors as with birth pangs. Jesus also used the same word picture — a mother in labor — to describe the trouble that would come upon the earth, including famines, increased wickedness, wars and earthquakes. Many take this to mean that those traumas to the earth and its inhabitants will increase in frequency and become more intense as the end of this era approaches. And that seems to be exactly what has been happening in the past few decades.

NO "END OF THE WORLD"

However, neither Jesus nor the New Testament writers actually predicted "the end of the world." This planet, created by God, will survive. But they clearly and emphatically predict that the world *as we know it* will end. Currently, Jesus is seated at the right side of God. But He is returning some day, in the human form in which He left earth, to bring judgment and order, and to establish His Kingdom.

For centuries God chose to deal with humankind through the Jews, His chosen people. But after He sent His Son, and that Son was rejected by the majority of the Jews, God began this "parenthetical period" in which we currently live. This is "the time of the Gentiles," in which God is calling believers from all nations and nationalities, making them a part of His Church, as a gift to His Son. But this current era will end some day and God will resume His special covenant with the Jews. Israel, and specifically Jerusalem, will become the capital of the world.

The "end will come," Jesus said, after the Gospel has been "preached in the whole world as a testimony to all nations." With the efforts of thousands of missionaries in the past 2000 years and the ability to spread the Gospel through radio, television, Internet, books, tapes and other media, that goal may already have been reached, or soon will be. Sometime thereafter, Jesus promises, He is returning to earth.

Jesus responds in Matthew 24 to the questions posed by His disciples, "When will this happen, and what will be the sign of your coming and the end of the age?" Only God the Father knows the day and hour Jesus will return, He stressed; He wants us to be constantly ready and watching for Him. In fact, Jesus says He "will come at an hour when you do not expect Him."

Jesus said that, before He returns to reign, there will be a time of "great distress, unequaled from the beginning of the world until now — and never to be equaled again." John, His beloved disciple, more fully describes this seven-year period, commonly known as the three-and-one-half year "Tribulation," followed by a second half, another three-and-one-half years, called "the Great Tribulation." Daniel, Isaiah, Jeremiah and other prophets also allude to this terrible period in which all of the world's problems come crashing to a grand crescendo, a horrible finale, and society reels out of control.

"Immediately after the distress of those days [the seven-year Tribulation]," Jesus told His followers, "the sun will be darkened, and the moon will not give its light; the stars will fall from the sky and the heavenly bodies will be shaken." (He was quoting Isaiah 13:10 and 31:4.) Again, more detail is found in the last book of the Bible, in which John writes about the forests and vegetation being burned, parts of the sea turning to blood, insect infestation, plagues, devastating wars, and other disasters. Large portions of the world's population will die and the survivors will wish they, too, were dead because of the plagues and other torments. So the foreboding feelings we may have about the earth, and about future society in general, are correct.

John also foresaw the end of this world's economic and false religious systems. Apparently, vigorous buying and selling will continue until the very end — the global economy may even improve, it infers — before a complete crash occurs. Then the merchants of the world will weep and mourn, terrified at this collapse which occurs "in one hour." The international economic network will suddenly become unplugged. This meltdown will make the worldwide Depression of the 1930s look like prosperity by comparison.

When Jesus returns, He will then judge the world and reign as its King for a thousand years, along with those who are martyred during the Tribulation. It is during this time that the prophets' predictions will come true, that Jesus shall judge among the nations, and they shall beat their swords into plowshares and their spears into pruning hooks, that there will be no more war, the "weak [will] say I am strong," and the meek shall finally inherit the earth.

Satan will be bound during those ten centuries, but will be released at its end "to deceive the nations" one more time, in a final, unsuccessful battle against Christ. Thereafter comes the "Great White Throne Judgment" in which all "the dead, great and small," will be "judged according to what they had done." "And if anyone's name was not found written in the Book of Life, he was thrown into the Lake of Fire," to join Satan and his rebellious followers, John prophesied, as if it has already occurred.

But even though our planet undergoes unbelievable war,

upheaval and destruction, *it does not end,* even at this point in the future. He who created it will supernaturally cleanse and restore the earth. Thereafter, John sees a "new heaven and a new earth."

Christ will then present the masterpiece which He has been building for us these past 2000 years. According to John's vision, "the New Jerusalem," also called "The Holy City," a diamond-like cube, 1400 cubic miles in size, will permanently hover above the newly restored earth. God Himself will reside there and His glory will be our light source, meaning that we will have no nighttime. This amazingly beautiful, jeweled city, beyond John's ability to describe, will be the eternal residence of those in Christ, His Church.

Inhabitants of this satellite "city" will be able to travel back and forth between it and this planet. The new earth will be different, apparently to accommodate a much larger population. For example, John says the oceans, which now cover three-fourths of the earth, will be no more. Perhaps the pre-Flood canopy of water vapor will be restored from the oceans into the atmosphere, which would provide an even climate and eliminate storms. And Isaiah foresaw that many mountains would be leveled, which would also allow more inhabitable land to accommodate a larger population.

So, as you can see, the Christian's New Testament does not claim that the planet itself is going to end. The world we see today, however, is not going to last forever in its present form.

SCOFFERS

Many scoff at the talk of a Second Coming of Jesus Christ, just as Peter predicted they would do. But, Peter notes, just as God stored waters in the atmosphere which He later unleashed in Noah's Flood, He will eventually bring a fiery destruction to all that is on Planet Earth. It's hard to imagine that the stock market, mansions, infrastructures, beautiful buildings, highways, monuments, great cruise ships, all of our great luxuries and earthly riches will someday be nothing but ashes. (And that is one reason why true Christians wish to store their treasures in Heaven, rather than here on Earth.)

FIRE INSURANCE

The good news is that we have an opportunity to reign with Jesus in that Millennial Kingdom. By accepting Him as Lord and Savior now, we can reside and even rule with Him in the new Heaven and Earth.

We can also escape the seven-year Great Tribulation. Peter wrote that "the Lord knows how to rescue godly men from trials." To the true and faithful Church Jesus promises, "I also will keep you from the hour of trial which shall come upon the whole earth, to test those who dwell on the earth." We know that God supernaturally removed Lot and his family from Sodom and Gomorrah before He judged those wicked cities by destroying them. He protected Noah and his family in the Ark during the judgmental worldwide Great Flood. And He will remove His true Church from this earth before He unleashes His wrath during the Great Tribulation. The wrath of God is reserved for unbelievers and the false church. But sincere and faithful believers "shall be saved from wrath" through Jesus Christ.

Many interpret the writings of Paul and other New Testament writers to indicate that Christians living just prior to that Tribulation period will be "caught up together...in the clouds to meet the Lord in the air," along with the dead in Christ, who will be resurrected. This supernatural, sudden departure from the world, sometimes called "the Rapture," is similar to what happened to Enoch in the Old Testament days.

This instantaneous removal of (possibly) millions of people from the earth will likely have the effect of causing many who are left behind to be converted to Christianity. They will suddenly realize that the prophecies they had heard about from those annoying Christians were absolutely true. Converts will undoubtedly also be made by the 144,000 missionaries who are redeemed and sealed by God in Israel in that time. Those courageous enough to be believers in Jesus Christ during that terrible time will suffer tremendous persecution. They will not be permitted to buy or sell. Many will be beheaded for attempting to spread the Gospel during that time. For Christians, it will be like the Roman Empire's persecution all over again, but worse. But whether a Christian or not, it will absolutely be the most terrible time ever to be living on Planet Earth. Read all about it sometime in the Book of Revelation.

LET'S PLAN FOR THE FUTURE

As the author of Hebrews writes, "How shall we escape if we ignore such a great salvation?" God has made the way of reconciliation uncomplicated and free, through faith in His son, Jesus Christ. We can be delivered from our sins and from eternal punishment by a simple act of placing our trust in Christ to save us.

And, for those of us who already consider ourselves to be true followers of Jesus Christ, we must constantly be "eager to make sure [our] calling and election [is] sure," Peter cautions. We should spend our lives seeking to do the will of God, not satisfying evil human desires, he urges. Adds Paul, we need to be on our guard, standing firm in the faith, strong and courageous, doing everything in love, and keeping a good conscience.

If we do this, we will be as the "five wise virgins" of Jesus' parable who took their lamps, wicks trimmed and full of oil, and went out to meet the bridegroom. Jesus ends that story by warning, "Therefore keep watch, because you do not know the day or the hour," in which He will return, and the world will never be the same. We don't know when the "Rapture" will occur; it could at any time.

So, although the planet survives, this world system is coming to an end. But a much better one awaits. And those who have put their faith in Jesus Christ can be optimistic, not pessimistic. As the old song goes, we've read the back of the book and we know how the story ends.

It's a very happy ending for Christians. **We *win!***

ALTAR CALL

At the end of most hellfire-and-brimstone sermons I have heard, the minister would give an "invitation" accompanied by a slow, mournful hymn such as "Just As I Am," or "Almost Persuaded." It seemed they would do their best to frighten someone into coming forward to accept Christ, telling scary stories about the one who procrastinated, only to be killed the next day in a car wreck.

I won't go into the long-term success rate of such emotionally-based "conversions." But it is worth noting that Jesus did not coerce, beg, plead or cajole people to follow Him, even though He knew Hell awaited those who refused. To the contrary, He warned many away, knowing their hearts. They weren't willing to abandon their self-centered lives in exchange for the eternal and abundant life He offered. At one point, only His disciples stuck with Him; the crowds had abandoned Him when they discovered the sacrifice and persecution that accompanied a life in Christ.

Do you know there is not even an example in the Bible of someone saying a "sinner's prayer" to accept Christ? Jesus' followers simply heard the Gospel message and accepted it — there is no mention of expressions of emotion, ceremony, or ritual.

God gave us logic as well as emotions. He wants us to use both as we make this decision — the most important we will ever consider. But expressing our need for God, our acceptance of His Son — whether from a church altar, one's vehicle, classroom, or hospital bed — is the traditional (and certainly appropriate) way to communicate with Him, whether in silent or audible prayer.

And it is clear from Scripture that the Holy Spirit must be at work in our minds and hearts for this Christian stuff to make any sense or be at all persuasive. Our spirits are dead, and must be resuscitated by the Spirit of God, or we are not even receptive to Him. Without that spark, it all seems like dry, ancient foolishness, appropriate only for the simple-minded, uneducated and superstitious, unworthy of our time and attention.

But if you've had that epiphany, and you do suddenly realize that you are a sinner in need of Christ, do not try to resist or "shake it off." Latch onto the invitation without delay and be thankful that God is offering it to you; it is a priceless gift. Again, the "pearl of great price," Jesus called it. He's not offering you just an escape from eternal Hell, which is reason enough to accept. He's also offering you a more abundant, fulfilling life, here and now.

So you have finally decided, "I have run out of excuses. I believe that there *is* a literal Heaven and Hell after this short life, as Jesus warned. I understand that I am a sinner and cannot save myself by doing good deeds. I put my trust fully in Jesus as my Lord and Savior. I strongly desire to give my life to Him and follow Him. Now what do I do next?"

First, He wants us to confirm what has happened inwardly, by an outward, public profession of faith, including water baptism. If we confess Him before men, He will confess us before His Father (Matt. 10:32-33).

Second, it is clear that He wants us to become *involved* in — not merely *attend* — a local assembly of Bible-believing Christians. We are to become a part of His body, using the talents He has given us, to advance His Kingdom. Believe it or not, there is something *each of us* has to offer to that local church that no one else can provide. There we can learn His Word, interact with other believers, and grow spiritually. Christ is the vine and we are His branches, drawing sustenance from Him.

Third, we must soak up the Word. When we read from the pages of the Bible, the Holy Spirit will illuminate our hearts and minds, helping the words begin to make sense and be credible, so that it will nourish our souls as food does our bodies. Like God who inspired it, the Bible's wisdom is an inexhaustible flow of "living water." You can study it a lifetime and, yet, still keep learning new principles until you die. Those Christians who do not "plug into" a local church, faithfully participating in a prayer and Bible study group, wither and become useless; their faith remains very weak.

Know that, despite your new life in Christ, temptation and difficulty do not abate; they may become more powerful than ever, in fact. That's another reason to stay plugged in. But if we flee from sin, even the very appearance of evil, God promises that He will help us handle it. He has guaranteed that we will never be subject to more temptation than we can resist. It helps, too, to make one's self accountable to fellow believers.

There is no need to fear that you will become a "Christian robot." Contrary to what some think, you *can* be a Christian and keep your own unique personality. In fact, the "real you" becomes more developed, more vibrant, as you submit to Jesus Christ.

Be confident in what you now possess. God will not take back that eternal life He has given you. You did not work for or earn it to begin with; there is no way you could possibly pay for it. Likewise, you do not *earn* the right to keep it; it is a *gift*. If Christ accomplished the greater work of dying for our sins and saving us, He certainly can accomplish the lesser work of *keeping* us. He promises that He will *never* leave us or forsake us, and that no one or nothing can separate us from His love. One of my favorite Bible passages is John 10:28-30, in which Jesus speaks of His sheep: "I give them eternal life, and they shall never perish; no one can snatch them out of My hand. My Father, who has given them to Me, is greater than all; no one can snatch them out of My Father's hand. I and the Father are One."

So if you *do* fall into sin as a believer, don't "wallow around in the mud" for a long time, as some are prone to do. Get up, confess it, turn away from it and go on, knowing God forgives you and that the penalty for that sin has already been paid by His Son.

God wants us to be "fishers of men" (Matthew 4:19). When Jesus called His disciples, He did not immediately tell them that He wanted to convey His wisdom to them or even command them to live a holy life, although He did eventually do both. His initial call was to proclaim the Good News to others, as He had done to them. Look for opportunities to share the Gospel with nonbelievers. After all, you needed someone to tell *you* about Jesus, right?

Last, Jesus asked Peter to "feed my sheep" (John 21:17). He wants us to disciple, encourage, and teach other believers, especially the young, weak or needy ones. We need to seek out opportunities to serve other people, showing kindness, friendship, generosity, hospitality, wisdom — anything we have to offer that they need. As you do so, you are acting as the hands and feet of your Lord. You will find such a pattern of giving to be immensely fulfilling and rewarding. It's what we are designed to do.

Contrary to the popular view of most outsiders, true Christians *enjoy* their new life. I have never known a long-time believer who ever regretted taking that path. In fact, just the opposite is true: many have said they wish they would have started sooner and thus avoided a lot of mistakes, heartache, and grief. Without Christ, life is essentially meaningless and the future is bleak. But a godly man's life, Proverbs 14:14 tells us, is satisfying. In The Living Bible translation, it says his life is *exciting*. That's been my experience: nothing is more satisfying, exciting, and meaningful than serving Christ.

Shall you begin your exciting journey today?

 Index

Anti-Christ 25, 75

Apostasy/Apostate 74, 75, 138

Deity 15, 17, 19, 22, 24, 25, 37, 44, 59, 74

Freedom 132, 133, 135

Grace 63, 70, 98, 101-103, 124, 126, 128

Intolerance 8, 74, 75, 105

Miracle(s) 17-19, 27, 37

Omnipresence 18

Omniscience 18

Peace 42, 109-112, 132, 137

Pentecost 24

Prophecy(ies) 32, 33, 45, 79, 137, 138

Rapture 142, 143

Repentance 62, 64

Sacrifice 39-42, 44-49, 64, 105, 118, 131

Salvation/Save 9, 43, 44, 48, 58, 62-64, 70, 78, 81, 87, 100-102, 105, 119, 120, 122, 124, 126, 130, 146

Self-control 58, 65, 67, 132

Temptation 110, 147

Tribulation 139, 140, 142

Works 100-102, 105, 126, 147

† Peace With God (New York, Permabooks, 1955, pp. 124–125.); Billy Graham

About The Author

Brad Crouser is a rather unique and versatile individual. He once managed and edited a weekly news magazine, *The Better Times Weekly*, which then was West Virginia's largest-circulating publication. During those early years he had private interviews with Ronald Reagan and Tony Blair, among other dignitaries.

After a few years as a newspaper editor and political columnist, he served in government, then began full-time practice of law in 1989. Today he is a distinguished author and a highly successful attorney. Over the years he has represented major national and international corporations.

Brad graduated Magna Cum Laude from the West Virginia University School of Journalism in 1976. He then obtained his Juris Doctorate Degree from the West Virginia University College of Law in 1979.

A noted speaker, he has lectured at a number of prominent universities, including West Virginia University, the University of Charleston and West Virginia University Institute of Technology, and at numerous seminars on a variety of legal subjects. Brad is occasionally a guest columnist for *The Charleston Daily Mail*, a statewide newspaper located in the state capital.

He was also named a Distinguished West Virginian in 1988.

He and his wife Sally have two children and are active at *Bible Center Church* in Charleston, West Virginia.

WOODLAND GOSPEL PUBLISHING

www.woodlandgospel.com

Check out some of our other Woodland Gospel titles:

The Authorized Biography of The Greenes
America's Southern Gospel Trio
Author Mike Collins
Hardbound

"The Greenes have proven time and time again that believers – even those who have given their lives to singing of God's faithfulness - face the same circumstances of life that everyone else does. But the hope and optimism they have found in Christ is a testimony to all of us who face dark days ... a testimony of victory through Jesus."
— Bill Gaither

Also, Pick Up Your Copy Of
Living The Good Life
By Dr. Charles M. Wood, II

Dr. Wood

With the heart-tugging charm reminiscent of titles like the original *Chicken Soup of the Soul*, this special softcover release from Woodland Gospel Publishing offers a variety of thought-provoking short stories and humorous yarns by pastor, professor, counselor, and newspaper columnist, Dr. Charles M. Wood, II.

"My father, Charles Wood, Sr., was an accomplished carpenter, who always worked with his calloused hands. As I remember him and his creative abilities, I realize that each one of his carpentry tools was important," Dr. Wood states in one chapter of this title.

"Each implement in Dad's tool belt performed a particular and necessary task. However, the tools couldn't perform the undertaking by themselves. They needed someone—a skilled and able craftsman—committed to putting them to good use."

Using his own words, Dr. Wood has himself become an accomplished craftsman in his own right, through his forty-plus years of ministry—an astute crafter of words. His tools: a keen observation of human behavior and a clever choice of words and anecdotal stories, which work together to create a collection of inspirational and often challenging messages.

Dr. Wood's wisdom and his perception of the human condition have been gleaned in the trenches, so to speak. Besides being a distinguished college professor in southern West Virginia, he has authored several textbooks, including Death And Dying For The Healthcare Worker, and he has been a Christian counselor for many, many years.

This is a book that gives practical advice on a variety of modern day issues. Without question, it's a volume that you'll want to read again and again.

Order your copy, or several copies, of *Living The Good Life* at www.woodlandgospel.com, or at www.bookworld.com.

---

www.woodlandgospel.com
The New Name In Christian Literature

If you read and found *What's My Excuse* to be helpful in your walk with Christ, consider giving a copy of this important book to a friend. Order additional copies from:

Woodland Gospel Publishing
118 Woodland Dr., Suite 1101
Chapmanville, WV 25508
(304) 752-7500
www.woodlandgospel.com

What's My Excuse is also available at fine bookstores across the country.

CONTACT FORM

If you invited Christ into your heart while reading this volume, please contact us so that we can send you additional information to help you as you begin this wonderful, exciting new life in Him.

I recently accepted Christ as my personal Savior. Please send me additional free literature to assist my in my Christian walk.

NAME _____

ADDRESS _____

STATE _____ ZIP _____

E-mail _____

Send this form to:
Woodland Gospel Publishing
118 Woodland Drive
Chapmanville, WV 25508

Congratulations on your decision to follow Jesus. Please allow several weeks to receive your packet.

Manuscripts or corresondence may be submitted to Woodland Gospel Publishing, Attention Submissions, 118 Woodland Drive, Chapmanville, WV 25508 . Allow up to 4 months on manuscript evaluation and response.

And we know that God causes all things to work together for good to those who love God, to those who are called according to His purpose. For those whom He foreknew, He also predestined to become conformed to the image of His Son, so that He would be the firstborn among many brethren; and these whom He predestined, He also called; and these whom He called, He also justified; and these whom He justified, He also glorified.

— Romans 8:28-30
(NASB)